ALPINE FLOWERS

About the Author

Gillian Price was born in England but moved to Australia when young. After taking a degree in anthropology and working in adult education, she set off to travel through Asia and trek the Himalayas. The culmination of her journey was Venice where, her enthusiasm fired for mountains, the next logical step was towards the Dolomites, only hours away. Starting there, Gillian is steadily exploring the mountain ranges and flatter bits of Italy and bringing them to life for visitors in a series of outstanding guides for Cicerone.

When not out walking with Nicola, her Venetian cartographer husband, Gillian works as a freelance travel writer www.gillianprice.eu. A committed promoter of public transport to minimise impact in alpine areas, she is an active member of the Italian Alpine Club CAI and Mountain Wilderness.

Other Cicerone guides by the author

Across the Eastern Alps – the E5
Gran Paradiso: Alta Via 2 Trek and Day Walks
Italy's Sibillini National Park
Shorter Walks in the Dolomites
Through the Italian Alps – the GTA
Trekking in the Alps (contributor)
Trekking in the Apennines – the GEA
Trekking in the Dolomites
Walking on the Amalfi Coast
Walking in the Central Italian Alps
Walking on Corsica
Walking in the Dolomites
Walks and Treks in the Maritime Alps
Walking in Sicily
Walking in Tuscany
Walking the Italian Lakes
Walking in Italy's Stelvio National Park

ALPINE FLOWERS

by Gillian Price

JUNIPER HOUSE, MURLEY MOSS,
OXENHOLME ROAD, KENDAL, CUMBRIA LA9 7RL
www.cicerone.co.uk

© Gillian Price 2014
First edition 2014
ISBN: 978 1 85284 565 0
Reprinted 2019 (with updates)

Printed in China on responsibly sourced paper on behalf of Latitude Press Ltd.
A catalogue record for this book is available from the British Library.
All photographs are by the author unless otherwise stated.

Those who dislike mountains and are bored with plants need have no dealings with this volume.

Reginald Farrer *The Dolomites (1913)*

Dedication
For Betty, my dear mum and flower aficionado

Acknowledgements

Grazie mille to Nick for his patience and Jonathan for agreeing to publish. Thanks also to Anna Mazza for her flower books and common sense, Professor Giovanni Caniglia for his expert tips, Dorothy Grace for her meticulous editing and Clare Crooke for the lovely layout.

In terms of reference sources, I am indebted to *Alpine Flowers of Britain and Europe* (Collins 1995, Christopher Grey-Wilson and Marjorie Blamey), and the mammoth three-volume *Flora Alpina* encyclopaedia (Zanichelli 2004) compiled by a Swiss team (D Aeschimann, K Lauber, DM Moser, JP Theurillat), as well as Massimo Spampani and Bruno Berti for their inspiring articles in the *Alpi Venete* magazine. Last but not least, the websites www.actaplantarum.org and www.fiorialpini.net. Any mistakes are undeniably mine.

Front cover: (L to R) Top row: Alpine Aster, Coltsfoot, Cowberry, Dusky Cranesbill; second row: Carnic Lily, Alpine Snowbell, King of the Alps, Lady's Slipper Orchid; third row: Alpine Buttercup, Spring Gentian, Alpine Toadflax, Yellow Mountain Saxifrage; bottom row: Meadow Saffron, Orange Lily, Bear's ear, Bee Orchid

Back cover: This thistle has successfully attracted two pollen distributors

CONTENTS

GLOSSARY

anther	found at the tip of a filament, this is the pollen-bearing part of a stamen
basal	means the leaves sprout from the base of the plant, not from the stalk
bulbil	aerial bulbs born on the above-ground part of the plant
calyx	made up of sepals, this protective husk casing encloses a bud and opens up with the flower
endemic	not necessarily rare, but found only in a limited geographical area
filament	stalk-like part of the stamen which supports the anther
labiate	describes a flower divided into two parts that look like lips
palmate	leaves shaped like the outstretched palm of a hand, with separate lobes
pinnate	compound leaves structured like a feather with multiple leaflets arranged on either side of the stalk
sepal	like leaves and usually green, these make up the calyx
stamen	this is made up of a filament and anther and is the male part of the flower, producer of pollen
stigma	prominent tip of a style, the tube for transporting pollen to the ovaries – the female part of the flower

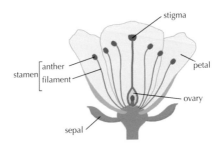

INTRODUCTION

Alpine Moon-daisy thrives in high rocky spots

Wild campanulas and purple gentians, deep gold Arnica blossoms, pink Daphne, and a whole world of other flowers, some quite new to us, here bloom in such abundance that the space of green sward on either side of the carriage-way looks as if bordered by a strip of Persian carpet.

Amelia Edwards Untrodden Peaks and Unfrequented Valleys:
A midsummer ramble in the Dolomites (1873)

It happens to all visitors to the European Alps – walkers, climbers and tourists alike. Engaged in a stiff climb, or a leisurely stroll along a mountain lane, and out of the corner of your eye you spot a curious flowering plant. It may even be vaguely reminiscent of something in the garden at home. And you store the image away: 'Must look that up when I get back'. The idea of this pocket guide is to act as a lightweight companion in the field, with colour-coded pages to make it easy to consult. With no pretence to be encyclopaedic, the guide focuses on the main flowers likely to be encountered and gives readers helpful pointers for distinguishing flowers that appear identical at first glance.

Colourful clumps of blooms make their home on 'meadows' of stone

Alpine flowers are unique, hardy species that appear brilliantly yet fleetingly during summer at high altitude. The challenges these tiny plants have to overcome are enormous: extreme temperatures, fierce winds, shortage or excess of moisture, thin soil, threat from livestock and humans and competition for reproduction. They need to do their utmost both to survive and to reproduce, and they have developed remarkably ingenious mechanisms to adapt to the range of stressful factors in their habitats. To say that alpine flowers have perfected survival techniques is an understatement!

SURVIVAL TECHNIQUES

The formidable mountainous barrier of the Alps begins close to sea level and soars to over 4000m, experiencing dramatic extremes of temperature. Cold is a crucial issue – for every 100m rise in altitude the thermometer drops by about 0.6°C. Moreover, there can be a 20–30°C difference in air temperature between day and night – and that's only at 2000m.

Challenges notwithstanding, a good 52 alpine flowers are known to survive up to 3500m above sea level, while an amazing 12 species make it to the 4000m mark. The record holder for altitude is the Glacier Crowfoot; an exemplar was reported on the 4274m Finsteraarhorn in the Swiss Bernese Alps. The leaf cells of the highest growing flowering plant in

Europe contain a high concentration of sugar which acts as an anti-freeze, lowering the freezing point of its tissues and thus enabling it to live amid snow and ice in sub-zero temperatures. Incredibly, the plant is able to photosynthesise even at -6°C.

Strange as it may seem at first, snow cover is essential to many alpine plants. It acts as a source of moisture and nutrients, but also provides protection from winds and extreme temperatures during the harsh winter months; however, it may mean they are under cover for eight months of the year. The air temperature drops dramatically, especially at night time, and when, for instance, the thermometer plunges to -33°C outside, snug under the snow it may be a comfortable -0.6°C, allowing the plant to function, albeit in a sort of hibernation. The Alpenrose seeks out north-facing slopes where snow accumulates to be sure of long-lasting blanket cover. Such plants can usually survive at temperatures as low as -25°C, which would seem amazing if it were not for the -70°C limit of plants that deliberately grow on windy crests! By contrast, dwellers in nooks and crannies on vertical rock faces, such as Devil's Claw and Moretti's Bellflower, cannot count on snow protection, but they are out of the range of chilling winds.

In spring as the white stuff starts to melt, light begins to filter downwards and triggers photosynthesis as the plant wakes up. Here the Alpine Snowbell comes into its own. One of the first blooms to appear in springtime, it can often be seen pushing its way up through the snow; in fact, the heat it releases as it breaks down carbohydrates can actually melt the snow.

Unstable terrain, such as the mobile scree slopes or talus found across the Alps, proves another challenge. Fragments of rock falling from higher rock faces and cliffs are constantly adding to the slopes, accumulating on the surface and provoking a downhill slide. A well-anchored root system is essential for any plant to be able to call such

The Alpine Snowbell pushes its way up through snow

terrain its home. Alpine Toadflax and Rhaetian Poppies are experts in this regard.

Survival techniques involving moisture are two-fold: retention and removal. Cactus-like succulents are experts at reducing moisture loss, with their thickly cuticled leaves, and they also have the ability to store water in their stems for times of need. The Cobweb Houseleek is true to its name and has a thick layer of soft netting on its rosettes, which additionally slows moisture loss from the plant's surface.

Small leaf size can effectively **minimise evaporation**, and a good example is Moss Campion. The technique used by the Edelweiss is to cover itself with white woolly hairs, which not only reduce moisture loss but also protect the plant from the strong solar radiation encountered at high altitudes. These hairs can also create a micro-climate around the plant where the temperature is slightly higher than that of the surrounding air.

In contrast, Lady's Mantle practises **guttation**, a process occurring under conditions of high humidity, particularly at night, whereby the plant exudes surplus water to the rim of its leaves. The drops of water are often mistaken for dew; these drops were treasured by ancient alchemists who claimed they could transform metals into gold – hence the genus name *Alchemilla*.

In a similar way, Saxifrage plants on limestone rock may find themselves overwhelmed by calcium salts. While the plant uses some for its

Calcium salt encrustations on Saxifrage leaves

physiological require-
ments, it banishes the
excess to the edges of its
leaves, and the resulting
encrustations have the
bonus effect of reinforcing
the leaf itself.

Keeping a **low profile**
as a protection from the
elements is a successfully
tried and tested technique
used by the likes of Alpine
Rock Jasmine, which
barely attains a height of
3 cm. However, below
the ground it develops a
root system that serves
as an anchor, penetrating
all available cracks in the
rock. Saxifrages are also
renowned specialists in

*Moss Campion produces a cushion where
small creatures can live*

this. With a genus name that means 'stone-breaker', the roots do just that,
fracturing the rock into particles and delving down, providing stability for
the plant while also on a quest for moisture. A number of prostrate woody
shrubs such as Retuse-leaved Willow have networks of slender roots and
branches that creep over rock surfaces, acting as anchors.

Moss Campion grows painstakingly slowly over its 20–30-year lifes-
pan, producing a woolly cushion rich in humus where small creatures
can live. Another plant that takes its time is Alpenrose, which needs 8–10
years for its seeds to mature into flowering plants. Then there's Net-leaved
Willow: it has been calculated that a trunk as slender as 7 mm could be 40
years old. Nature outclasses the bonsai masters!

Many alpine plants practise **solar tracking**, which is also known by
the rather forbidding term of heliotropism. In addition to placing their
leaves perpendicular to the sun's rays to maximise exposure and encourage photosynthesis, they make constant alterations to the angle of their
flower heads so as to receive the full blast of the sun's warming rays all

day long. Buttercups with their yellow saucers are experts in this field; they are able to store heat and the temperature inside the petals can be 8°C hotter than the surrounding air: a great lure for insects that need warm conditions as well as a boost for the plant itself as seed development accelerates. Should the heat become overwhelming, the plant can rotate its 'satellite dish' parallel to the incoming rays to reduce exposure; this also minimises moisture loss, essential in dry habitats.

The Carline Thistle, on the other hand, has the advantage of **hygrometric (moisture measuring) equipment** in the scales that envelop its flowers. This is triggered in adverse weather and the flower closes up in self-defence; it will then open when conditions improve. This behaviour has earned the plant the reputation of being a reliable weather forecaster.

REPRODUCTION

In their very short annual growth period, concentrated into 100 days at most, survival is not the sole life purpose of alpine flowers; reproduction is also crucial. Generally speaking, a plant's growth period and opportunity to reproduce is shortened by a week for every 100m of altitude. A mind-boggling array of techniques has been invented by flowering plants in order to encourage pollination and spread their seeds, and competition can be fierce.

A Painted Lady butterfly with Round-leaved Pennycress

Attracting insects

Colour is a key factor in attracting insects which, while feeding, inadvertently gather pollen and spread it, thus improving the plant's chances of reproduction. Many alpine flowers only bloom for the two midsummer months of July and August, and the plants make the most of it with a brilliant display of livery.

Dominant colours at high altitudes are red and purple, but there are lots of blue and yellow flowers and also a multitude of white and green flowers: the pale Edelweiss is a good example.

Bees evidently prefer blooms of pink, blue and yellow and keep a special eye out for flowers with distinctive patterns. They are also suited to flowers with closed or unusual shapes which are fairly sturdy so they can clamber inside.

Insect orchids give pollinators an additional helping hand. The Bee Orchid, for instance, fools bees into thinking they have found a mate, and as they alight the pollen rubs off onto their back to be carried away. The Lady's Slipper Orchid, on the other hand, entices potential pollinators into its cavity and then makes it hard for them to clamber out again, because of its slippery walls and in-turned lips. In the ensuing struggle they become coated with pollen, which they then carry with them to the next flower.

Cottongrass seeds are attached to a fluffy lightweight head

Flies have weaker vision, reportedly going for bright white and yellow flowers and flatter, saucer-shaped blooms on which they can land without complication. Butterflies, by contrast, have long, thin feeding gear so they prefer tubular flowers. Beetles reportedly like strongly scented flowers as well as bright colours.

Seed dispersal

An important system of seed transport and dispersal – the wind – is exploited by alpine flowers to maximum effect. Cottongrass plants attach their seeds to a fluffy lightweight head that is easily detached and carried off by a breeze.

Other flowers have another card up their sleeve to double their chances of reproducing and seeing another summer. Two notable examples are the Orange Lily and the Alpine Bistort which carry a multitude of 'bulbils' or aerial bulbs down their stem; these drop to the ground and mature after two or three years. Similarly, the Cobweb Houseleek has rosettes that can be dropped, propelled by the wind they roll away to a new spot to begin another colony.

Gaining nutrients

Insectivorous plants such as the Butterworts exploit insects in a different way – by eating them! Their sticky leaves act as old-fashioned flypaper, trapping the insects. The victims are digested over two days, supplying the host with essential nitrogen and phosphorous and the remains are left on the leaves to be washed away by rain or dew.

Some plants steal to gain the nutrients they need for survival. The Broomrapes, which do not contain chlorophyll and cannot produce their own food, are parasites that tap into the roots of other plants.

Predators

A particular threat to alpine flora is posed by living creatures. Chamois enjoy nibbling Leopardsbane (known as 'Chamois Grass' in German), evidently for its high sugar content, while marmots have a penchant for Forget-me-nots. Some human beings continue the unfortunate practice of picking blooms; it was once the fashion to press them between the pages of a book. Fortunately, most enlightened modern-day visitors take away only photographs. Not only does this preserve the brilliance of the colours, it is also the perfect way to appreciate them. It means, for instance, that the picture can be enlarged, revealing previously invisible aspects of these fascinating and precious plants.

Many of the flowers in this guide are protected – the Edelweiss was the very first, thanks to an 1836 law in Austria. Some, like the Lady's Slipper Orchid, are already rare and risk extinction. It goes without saying that all alpine wild flowers should be left in their natural habitat for others to wonder at.

MIGRATION AND CLIMATE CHANGE

The origin of a number of alpine species has been traced to the Arctic region and the freezing steppes of central Asia. With the advance of glaciers during the Ice Ages they migrated southwards, spreading out in search of less demanding conditions, and then staying on after the retreat of the icy masses. Well-known examples are the Edelweiss and the Net-leaved Willow.

Nowadays, with ongoing climate change the Alps, as everywhere, are feeling the effects of the progressive rise in global temperature. Glaciers and snow fields are reducing in surface area, sometimes quite drastically, and the vegetation is shifting upwards in altitude as the plants do their best

Alpine Squill and White Crocus appear in springtime

to seek optimum conditions for growth and survival. The Alpine regions are seeing the arrival of plants previously found lower down on the plains. Monitoring shows that the fastest can ascend 35m in three years. For more see www.gloria.ac.at.

NAMING

The scientific names for flowers can be quite intimidating, but they are both essential and intriguing in their references. Swedish doctor and naturalist Carl Linnaeus (1707–1778) introduced the classification system whereby each name consists of two Latin parts, both usually written in italics. The first, beginning with a capital letter, is the *Genus* (*Genera* is the plural form), referring to a group of closely related species. This is followed by the actual species name, starting with a small letter, used for members of a group that can inter-breed; this is referred to as the 'tag' in the plant descriptions in this guide.

An even larger grouping is the family, a looser grouping of genera that share common features such as flower shape or number of petals that distinguish them from others; examples are the Daisy and Pink families.

Naturally, plants all over the Alps have been given common or 'vulgar' names which are much easier for non-experts to remember. As an example, Queen of the Alps is the common name for *Eryngium* (genus name) *alpinum* (species or tag). For the purposes of this guide an English name (as well as the Latin name) has been used as the main reference and in the Flower Index, but names in French, German and Italian are also listed for each flower to aid walkers across the whole of the Alps.

These common names often provide a fascinating insight into local beliefs and age-old legends. The example *par excellence* is again the Edelweiss, German for 'noble white' from the story of a maiden who resolved to remain pure, and transmuted into the bloom on death. A second explanation comes from the Italian Dolomites, where they say the flower was tailor-made for a princess pining away for her pale homeland, the moon.

IDENTIFICATION

For the purposes of this book, the altitude of 1500m above sea level has been taken as the cut-off level for alpine flowers, although the odd exception found lower down and considered to be of special interest has been included.

The primary method of identification used here is colour, and to make flower recognition quick and easy – the aim of this guide – flowers have been grouped together under their dominant colour. Naturally, there are infinite variations in shades of colour, especially with blues, reds and purples, so it is always a good idea to leaf through other sections when searching for a flower.

The colours are presented in the following order in this book:

- RED: shades from pink to red and burgundy
- YELLOW: covering the range through to orange
- BLUE: from light hues through to royal blue
- PURPLE: delicate lilac to rich purple charged with blue and red
- WHITE: predominantly white or creamish. Green has also been included here

and alphabetically by their English name within each colour section.

As well as a photograph, key characteristics of each flower are briefly described in simple language for (and by) the non-expert. Notes on name derivation and traditional uses are included. Specialised terminology has been purposely kept to a minimum; however, some terms are necessary for distinguishing similar species and to help observation and identification. **Note** Even the leading authoritative reference guides disagree on the identification of some plants so there may well be differences of opinion for the flowers in this guide as well.

Each individual flower heading shows the name in English and then, underneath, in Latin (in italics), then French, German and Italian.

A Glossary and a simplified diagram of a flower are also provided at the front of the book, after the contents page.

DISTRIBUTION

If not specified in the individual description, the flowers are found widely across the Alps.

There is a marvellous network of botanical gardens across the length and breadth of the Alpine chain, in Austria, France, Italy, Slovenia and Switzerland. Each has expertly labelled species, which is of great help for interested visitors. A list is given in the Appendix.

FLOWERS

This thistle has successfully attracted two pollen distributors

Alpenrose

Rhododendron ferrugineum – Rhododendron ferrugineux –
Rostblättrige Alpenrose – Rododendro ferrugineo

Thickets of this attractive evergreen shrub cover vast swathes of mountain-sides up to 3200m altitude, often in the company of larch and bilberries. The name derives from the Greek 'tree of roses' and it puts on a glorious show June–August with clusters of pink-red bell-shaped blooms. It can be distinguished from the otherwise identical Hairy Alpenrose by rusty-coloured scales underneath its shiny dark green leaves. These contain toxic substances, a savvy protection from grazing livestock. Its dried branches were once fashioned into brooms or used to filter milk.

Alpine Aster

Aster alpinus – Aste des Alpes – Alpen-Aster – Astro alpino

A striking member of the Daisy family that brightens alpine pastures and dry stony places with its pinkish or, less commonly, mauve outer petals and rich yellow disc-like heart. It grows as high as 3200m altitude, and flowers June–August. Aster comes from the Greek for 'star'.

Alpine Gypsophila, Creeping Baby's Breath

Gypsophila repens – Gypsophile rampante –
Kriechendes Gipskraut – Gipsofila strisciante

A sprawling clump of silvery grey leaves all but smothered with tiny stars of pale pink or lilac. On close inspection five-petalled flowers with minimal notches are revealed. It flowers May–August and prefers dry stony places and bare rock surfaces up to 2900m altitude. The main name means 'lover of chalk' while the tag is 'creep' and in fact the stems are semi-prostrate.

Alpine Rock-jasmine

Androsace alpina – Androsace des Alpes –
Alpen-Mannschild – Androsace alpina

An eye-catching spreading cushion plant that hugs screes and rock surfaces, keeping as low a profile as possible. Very small pretty pale pink or white flowers with five petals are accompanied by lance-shaped leaves covered in short hairs. Unlike the very similar Moss Campion, this has rounded petals and a yellowish centre, as well as woody branches and roots. Widespread, it flowers July–August as high as 4000m altitude.

Alpine Rose

Rosa pendulina – Rosier des Alpes – Alpen-Heckenrose –
Rosa alpina

An exceptionally pretty pinkish-purple rose that grows in dense thickets that emanate a recognisable sweet fragrance. The flower centre is white, punctuated with showy yellow anthers. The bushes can grow as tall as 2m and do not generally have thorns. It flowers June–July in clearings and woodland up to 2600m altitude.

Alpine Thrift, Mountain Thrift

Armeria alpina – Arméria des Alpes – Alpen-Grasnelke –
Armeria alpina

Just like the seaside version – in fact the name may derive from the Celtic for 'near the sea' – this thrift is a multibloom tuft atop a slender hairless green stalk, accompanied by slim spiky leaves. The calyx resembles thin plastic sheeting and embraces a bunch of flowers ranging from bright to pale pink. Its habitat is screes and damp meadows up to 3100m, and it flowers July–August across all but the central-north Alps.

Alpine Willowherb

Epilobium fleischeri – Épilobe de Fleischer –
Kies-Weidenröschen – Epilobio di Fleischer

While similar to Rosebay Willowherb, this plant is blunter in shape and notably shorter. It bears paler pink flowers distinguished by dark pink stamens. It flowers July–September up to 2700m altitude on moraines and river banks and is widespread with the exception of the eastern Alps.

Bee Orchid

Ophrys apifera – Ophrys abeille –
Bienen-Ragwurz – Ofride fior d'ape

Just one of the weird and wonderful so-called insect orchids, this resembles a bee. The exquisite flowers have pink-purple outer lips framing a deep brown velvet man-like figure. It flowers May–June on grassy places in patches across the Alps up to 1800m altitude. *See also* other orchids: Black Vanilla; Yellow: Elder-flowered and Lady's Slipper; Purple: Broad-leaved Marsh, Common Spotted and Heath Spotted; White: Burnt, Musk and Small White.

Bird's-eye Primrose

Primula farinosa – Primevère farineuse –
Mehl-Primel – Primula farinosa

This dainty Primrose has a multitude of light pink-lilac flowers, each with five toothed petals and a tiny yellow eye, atop a slender stalk. Sprouting from the base are pale grey-green veined leaves that contain a white farinaceous powder. It flowers May–August on marshes and damp meadows up to 3000m altitude. *See also* Stinking Primrose; Yellow: Bear's-ear, Oxlip and Primrose; Purple: Marginate Primrose.

Black Vanilla Orchid

Nigritella nigra – Orchis vanillé – Schwarzes Männertreu –
Nigritella comune

Rich alpine meadows are often dotted with tiny dark brown-reddish orchids that go unnoticed by the uninitiated eye. Close up, the surprisingly strong vanilla-cocoa scent is evident and according to alpine hearsay, cows that eat them produce chocolate-flavoured milk! The flower can be rounded or pyramidal and also comes in pink. It flowers June–August up to 2800m altitude. *See also* other orchids: Bee; Yellow: Elder-flowered and Lady's Slipper; Purple: Broad-leaved Marsh, Common Spotted and Heath Spotted; White: Burnt, Musk and Small White.

Carthusian Pink

Dianthus carthusianorum – Oeillet des Chartreux –
Gewöhnliche Karthäuser-Nelke – Garofano dei Certosini

Thin leaves are placed at intervals on tall slender stalks that bear dense clusters of vivid deep pink-purple flowers with a central patch of white, serrated petals and a brown-purple calyx. It flowers May–August to 2500m altitude across most of the Alps. Dianthus derives from the ancient Greek for 'flower of the Gods', although 'Pink' was probably first used for the flower and later extended to the colour. The plant was popular in Roman times for ceremonies, while the Arabs appreciated its scented species for distilling perfume; no wonder the Crusaders brought it back to Europe. *See also* Large, Maiden and Three-veined Pink.

Catsfoot, Mountain Everlasting, Cudweed

Antennaria dioica – Pied de chat dioïque –
Gewöhnliches Katzenpfötchen – Antennaria dioica

Unusual pale pink, reddish or white flowers with multiple petals surrounding a darker centre punctuated with multiple protruding stamens. The stalks are long and thick and several leaves attached, though the majority are around the base, silvery grey and oval. The plant is reportedly helpful in treating gastric ailments. Commonly found, it flowers June–August on dry heaths, rocks and meadows up to 3000m altitude.

Caucasian Stonecrop

Sedum spurium – Orpin bâtard – Kaukasus-Fetthenne –
Sedo del Caucaso

This plant originally hailed from the Caucasus region but is now naturalised across the Alps, with the exception of the southwest. Its fleshy rounded leaves form open rosettes and attractive white-red or pink star-shaped flowers tightly grouped together. It grows in dense carpets on stony wastes up to 1800m altitude, and flowers June–August. The genus name derives from the Latin for 'settle' as the leaves of some species are believed to bring relief for wounds. As Stonecrops are commonly found on walls and roofs, they were popularly believed to protect houses from lightning strikes and fires. *See also* Yellow: Biting and Creamish Stonecrop; White: Thick-leaved Stonecrop.

Cobweb House-leek

Sempervivum arachnoideum – Joubarbe aranéeuse –
Filzige Spinnweb-Hauswurz – Semprevivo ragnateloso

Minuscule leaf rosettes coated in a cobweb of down typify this succulent. A lover of rocky crannies and dry but sun-blessed terrain, it grows at 1700–3000m altitude. By far the brightest of its kind, its brilliant red star flowers may be streaked with purplish pink, on reddish-brown stalks. As with the other house-leeks, in addition to resembling a triffid, it holds true to the sempervivum (ever alive) designation and does not die back during winter. It flowers July–September. *See also* Common and Mountain House-leek; Yellow: Wulfen's House-leek.

Common Bistort

Polygonum bistorta – Renouée bistorte –
Schlangen-Knöterich – Poligono bistorta

Meadows smothered with
pink-tipped spikes are a common foreground to the Alps.
These spikes bear a tight
cluster of tiny flowers that
sway in the breeze, and long
oval leaves grow alongside.
The strange name refers to its
'many-kneed' jointed root.
It flowers at length May–
September up to 2500m altitude. *See also* White: Alpine
Bistort.

Common House-leek

Sempervivum tectorum – Joubarbe des toits –
Dach-Hauswurz – Semprevivo dei tetti

Dull pink flowers with a yellow centre and a perfectly circular display
of delicate stamens distinguish this
evergreen House-leek. A large tall
plant, it has an especially stocky stalk
tinged reddish-brown and smallish
blue-green-red basal rosettes. It is distributed in large patches across most
of the Alps, except for the northeast. It
flowers June–September on grassy
and rocky terrain up to 2800m altitude. *See also* Cobweb and Mountain
House-leek; Yellow: Wulfen's
House-leek.

Common Lungwort

Pulmonaria officinalis – Pulmonaire officinale –
Echtes Lungenkraut – Polmonaria officinale

The crepe-like flowers begin life pink
but gradually assume a bluish-purple
hue, so the plant often sports dual
colours. It has long been used in the
treatment of coughs and lung ailments.
The leaves are hairy with large light
blotches and shaped like elongated
hearts. It flowers in damp woods
March–May up to 1900m altitude, and
is widespread except for the eastern
Alps.

Cowberry

Vaccinium vitis-idaea – Airelle rouge –
Preiselbeere – Mirtillo rosso

Delicate white, open bell-shaped blooms of the cowberry are followed
by the edible though acidic-tasting red berry fruit which appears at the
end of summer. A miniature evergreen shrub, it has an extensive system
of underground roots, and flowers May–August up to 3000m altitude
on open heath, woods and pastures, often in the company of the tastier
Blueberry.

Creeping Azalea, Alpine Azalea

Loiseleuria procumbens – Azalée des Alpes – Alpenazalee –
Azalea delle Alpi

Clusters of minuscule light pink flowers shaped like bells grow amongst dark green oblong leaves with rolled edges. A woody shrub, it forms extensive mats that hug the ground, hence the tag which means 'prostrate'. While not terribly common, it is found across the Alps up to 3000m altitude on dry rocky terrain often in windswept spots, and flowers June–July. The plant's reduced dimensions and ground hugging profile make it easy to distinguish from similar Dwarf Alpenrose.

Cyclamen, Sowbread

Cyclamen purpurascens – Cyclamen pourpre –
Europäisches Alpenveilchen – Ciclamino delle Alpi

A beautiful plant with deep purple-carmine nodding flowers. Its heart-shaped leaves are dark green and glossy with light vein tracings. The common English name derives from the Medieval Latin, a reminder that it was swine feed, whereas the Cyclamen family name comes from the Greek for 'circle', plausibly due to the round tuber. It flourishes in well-shaded damp woods, especially beech, and flowers July–September as high as 1800m altitude. It is found everywhere but the far southern Alps.

Dwarf Alpenrose, Ground Cistus

Rhodothamnus chamaecistus – Rhodothamne ciste nain –
Zwergalpenrose – Rododendro cistino

This is exactly what the name says – a dwarf version of the attractive and wide-spread Alpenrose. The low-lying woody shrub has hairy branches and very small tough leaves that are bright green. The flower has five separate pale pink petals but its distinguishing feature are the showy long white filaments that end in dark brown anthers surrounding a pink stigma. It flowers May–July across the eastern Alps on dry open slopes and rock surfaces up to 2400m altitude. An even smaller similar plant is prostrate Creeping Azalea.

Dwarf Soapwort, Pygmy Soapwort

Saponaria pumila – Niedriges Seifenkraut –
Saponaire naine – Saponaria minore

The pretty deep rose pink flowers with five separate notched petals are more or less stemless. They sprout from a cushion crowded with small fleshy oblong leaves. The low plant spreads across meadows and rocky terrain. A rare find, it grows in the central-eastern Alps up to 2600m altitude. It flowers July–September. The tag means 'dwarf'. *See also* Rock Soapwort, which has rather smaller flowers.

Dwarf Valerian

Valeriana supina – Valériane naine – Zwerg-Baldrian –
Valeriana sdraiata

The unusual eye-catching plant forms attractive thick carpets composed of posies of delicate pink flowers. These nestle in a tight mesh of light green oblong leaves, whose edges are turned inwards like scoops. It flowers July–August up to 2900m altitude on rocks and screes, often close to snow. Valerian may be dedicated to Roman emperor Galerius Valerius who prescribed it for insomnia, though it was Hippocrates in the 4th century BC who described its hypnotic effect. It was also well known to the Mayans. *See also* Red Valerian.

Hairy Alpenrose

Rhododendron hirsuta – Rhododendron cilié –
Bewimperte Alpenrose – Rododendro irsuto

This miniature rhododendron shrub smothered in pretty pink bell-shaped flowers forms evergreen thickets across mountainsides and open woods. Unlike the similar and more common Alpenrose, this has dark green leaves that are both hairy and shiny, and it is also slightly lower in stature. It is found up to 2600m across the Alps with the exception of the western regions, and flowers May–July.

Hoary Plantain

Plantago media – Plantain moyen – Mittlerer Wegerich –
Piantaggine media

Plantains are common countryside plants with some 200 types in the genus, but this one grows as high as 2450m altitude across the Alps and is easily recognisable by its pretty pink-lilac hue. Tall spikes carry rather inconspicuous and mildly fragrant flowerheads comprising long filaments tipped with a white-brown anther. The oval leaves are ribbed and downy, and grouped around the base of the stalk in a rosette formation. It flowers May–September on stony terrain. Its medicinal applications from olden times range from the treatment of toothache to constipation.

Large Pink

Dianthus superbus – Oeillet superbe – Gewöhnliche Pracht-Nelke –
Garofano superbo

Simply superb, these pretty pink flowers with long straggly fringed edges share a branched stalk with slender leaves like blades of grass. Producing a delicate scent, it flowers June–September up to 2400m altitude in patches over most of the Alps. *See also* Carthusian, Maiden and Three-veined Pink.

Maiden Pink

Dianthus deltoides – Oeillet à delta – Heide-Nelke –
Garofano deltoide

The deep pink flower of this attractive Pink is recognisable by a darker coloured central ring along with faint spotting across the petals. It is has no fragrance to speak of and grows in dry sun-blessed meadows and open woods up to an altitude of 2000m. It is widely distributed across all but the central Alps and flowers June–September. *See also* Carthusian, Large and Three-veined Pink.

Martagon Lily, Turk's Cap Lily

Lilium martagon – Lis martagon – Türkenbund – Giglio martagone

A magnificent lily found all over the Alps, this is immediately recognisable by its gorgeous wine-red blooms with dark spots. The petals curve backwards into a distinctive shape – in fact the martagon tag derives from the Turkish for turban or cap – and it features prominent stamens. It flowers June–July in meadows and open woods up to 2800m altitude. *See also* Yellow: Carnic and Lesser Turk's Cap Lily.

Mezereon

Daphne mezereum – Daphné mézéréon – Gewöhnlicher Seidelbast –
Fior di stecco

This well-known shrub produces heavenly scented flowers that grow straight out of bare twigs, sometimes in the company of unassuming bunches of pale green oblong leaves. It flowers at length February–July, after which come bright red berries. It is found in woods and alpine meadows up to 2600m altitude. As with all Daphnes – whose name derives from Greek for 'laurel', reportedly for leaf similarity – the plant is toxic. As if to reinforce this the name tag may derive from the Persian for 'poison'. *See also* Striped Daphne; White: Alpine Mezereon.

Moss Campion

Silene acaulis – Silène acaule – Kalk-Polsternelke – Silene acaule

Dubbed 'marmot bread', cushions of bright green leaves dotted with tiny pink blooms thrive on apparently barren stony surfaces. Unlike the very similar Alpine Rock-jasmine, Moss Campion is neither woody nor hairy, while the flowers have toothed petals and noticeable white stamens rather than a yellow centre. It flowers June–August and lives on damp screes and rocks up to 3700m altitude. The genus was named after the aged woodland satyr Silenus who hung out with Dionysus (*aka* Bacchus) – Linnaeus evidently drew a parallel between the swollen flower-bearing capsules and his bald head and wine-bloated belly! *See also* Rock Campion; White: Bladder Campion.

Mountain House-leek

Sempervivum montanum – Joubarbe des montagnes –
Gewöhnliche Berg-Hauswurz – Semprevivo montano

Another fascinating triffid-like member of the Sempervivum family, this house-leek is hairy and sports pointed pinkish flowers and a dull yellow centre. It stays close to the ground, reaching a maximum height of 15cm, and the basal rosettes may be red-tipped. It flowers July–September on stony ground and screes up 3200m altitude. *See also* Cobweb and Common House-leek; Yellow: Wulfen's House-leek.

Peony

Paeonia officinalis – Pivoine officinale –
Gebräuchliche Pfingstrose – Peonia officinale

Magnificent vermilion cup-shaped flowers adorn bushy plants as tall as 100cm, forming clumps in woods and shaded meadows. The flimsy blooms only last for a matter of days, quickly drooping to expose the yellow stamens. It took its name from Paeon, a student of the great Greek god of medicine, Asclepius, who turned on him in a fit of jealous wrath after he successfully cured Mars and Pluto.

Luckily Zeus stepped in and transformed him into the flower. The peony was widely used in medicine until the 16th century to treat epilepsy, headaches and kidney stones, while as a potent magic it rid homes of demons, ensured pleasant dreams and provided birth control. It flowers May–June across the central-southern Alps to 1800m altitude.

Pink Cinquefoil

Potentilla nitida – Potentille luissant – Dolomiten-Fingerkraut – Potentilla rosea

Gorgeous dense cushions of pink flowers amid silvery green leaves cascade over bare rocks in the south-eastern Alps. It is easy to recognise by its distinctive colouring and five-petal formation around a darker red heart. Potentilla derives from 'strong' to reflect the plant's resilience; the term was coined by Renaissance botanists to emphasise its medicinal qualities and success in colonisation. It flowers June–September up to 3200m altitude. *See also* White: Lax Potentilla.

Purple Lychnis

Lychnis flos-jovis – Silène fleur de Jupiter – Jupiter-Lichtnelke – Silene fior di Giove

The long greyish-green stems are covered with fine white hairs, and crowned with bright pink-purple flowers in dense clusters. Lower down are pairs of small leaves. Lychnis comes from 'lantern' as the ancient Greeks fashioned the stalks into wicks, while the tag is 'flower of Jupiter'. (It is also known as *Silene flos-jovis*.) It flowers June–July on rocky terrain and meadows up to 2100m altitude across the central and western Alps.

Red Valerian

Centranthus ruber – Centranthe rouge – Rote Spronblume –
Valeriana rossa

Also known as *Valeriana rubra*, this showy bushy plant grows up to a metre in height. Its habitat embraces stony wastelands, old masonry walls and even roadsides. It flowers May–September to around the 1400m altitude mark, and has been included here as it is encountered widely across all but the central-north and north-eastern Alps. This plant was once attributed with magical powers: its roots would be dried and crushed and kept in a drawer to protect a home from lightning strikes. *See also* Dwarf Valerian.

Rock Campion

Silene rupestris – Silène des roches – Felsen-Leimkraut – Silene rupestre

The tiny notched five-petalled flowers come in a delicate pale pink or white. Greyish-green branched stalks and small oval leaves complete the picture. It spreads over rocks and screes up to 2900m altitude, flowering June–August. *See also* Moss Campion; White: Bladder Campion.

Rock Cranesbill

Geranium macrorrhizum – Géranium à gros rhizome –
Grosswurzel-Storchschnabel – Geranio crestato

Lively reddish-lilac nodding flowers with round petals and bright green palmate leaves distinguish this plant. It grows in large spreads in shady woodland and on rocky terrain, flowering May–August across the south-eastern Alps to 2500m altitude. Geranium comes from the Greek for 'crane' due to the longish seed pod resembling the bird's beak. *See also* Silvery Cranesbill; Purple: Dusky and Wood Cranesbill.

Rock Soapwort

Saponaria ocymoides – Saponaire faux basilic –
Rotes Seifenkraut – Saponaria rossa

This is a sprawling hairy plant with tiny pretty bright pink five-petalled flowers. It is rather similar to Moss Campion and Alpine Rock-jasmine but the petals are quite separate and the leaves more elongated – rather like basil according to the French name tag. The species name refers to the 'soap' property of the roots. It flowers May–September everywhere except the far northeastern Alps, up to 2000m altitude. *See also* Dwarf Soapwort, whose flowers are larger, despite the name.

Rosebay Willowherb

Epilobium angustifolium – Épilobe à feuilles étroites –
Schmalblättriges Weidenröschen – Epilobio a foglie strette

This elegant plant with long pyramid-shaped inflorescences can grow to 2m in height. It is a symbol of hope, as it was one of the first flowering plants to sprout amid bombed-out ruins across Europe in the wake of the Second World War; it also spreads quickly over bare land where trees have recently been felled. In the Causasus the leaves are dried for tea. It blooms June–October in large showy colonies up to 2000m altitude. *See also* Alpine Willowherb, a smaller type.

Silvery Cranesbill

Geranium argenteum – Géranium argenté – Silber-Storchschnabel – Geranio argentato

With unusual delicate rose-pink blooms and striped dark veining, these notched five-petalled flowers look more like a poppy than a member of the Geranium family. The silvery grey leaves are sculpted into deep lobes. A rare plant only found in the south-western and south-eastern Alps, it flowers July–August on limestone terrain up to 2200m altitude. *See also* Rock Cranesbill; Purple: Dusky and Wood Cranesbill.

Slender Broomrape

Orobanche gracilis – Orobanche grêle – Zierliche Sommerwurz –
Orobanche gracile

On first glance this would appear to be an orchid, with its upright stem and the shape of its flowers. However this bizarre flowering plant is a parasite, reaping nourishment from the roots of legumes – the name derives from the Greek for 'strangle legume'. It lacks green pigment, but comes in an unusual red-golden colour. It is found across the Alps on rich meadows up to 2000m altitude, flowering May–August. *See also* Yellow: Light Yellow Broomrape.

Stinking Primrose

Primula hirsuta – Primevère hérissée – Rote Felsen-Primel –
Primula irsuta

With flowers that are bright pink-purple, almost crimson, with a large white eye, this primrose is hard to miss. The blooms rise in bunches from fleshy round leaves that are slightly toothed. It flowers at length April–July across all but the eastern Alps on stony terrain as high as 3600m altitude. *See also* Bird's-eye Primrose; Yellow: Bear's-ear, Oxlip and Primrose; Purple: Marginate Primrose.

Striped Daphne

Daphne striata – Daphné strié – Gestreifter Seidelbast – Dafne striata

Exquisite scented pink-reddish posies of small waxy tube flowers reminiscent of cloves, leave little room on the prostrate evergreen shrub for leaves. These come in bunches, blunt bright green and lance-like, rather like flattened conifer needles. It prefers stony places and woods up to 2900m altitude, flowering May–August in the central and south-eastern Alps, with patches in the west. Bright red berries appear at the end of summer. *See also* Mezereon; White: Alpine Mezereon.

Three-veined Pink

Dianthus neglectus or *Dianthus pavonius* – Oeillet oeil de paon – Pfaun-Nelke – Garofano pavonio

Another pretty Pink though with no scent, this one can be recognised by its dark centre, three faint veins on the petals and the green-white colouring on the underside of the flower. It bears the typical slender leaves and grows in sunny spots as high as 3000m altitude in the western Alps. It flowers July–August. *See also* Carthusian, Large, Maiden and Wood Pink.

Two-flowered Saxifrage

Saxifraga biflora – Saxifrage à deux fluers – Zweitblütiger Steinbrech – Sassifraga biflora

Brilliant reddish-purple flowers peek from chinks in broken rock scree and moraines at altitudes as high as 3200m. A hardy plant, it has five tiny separate petals around a large yellow centre and very small tight leaf rosettes. It flowers June–August across most of the Alps except for the east, south and far western parts. The genus name means 'rock breaker', though it may allude to a former application for dissolving kidney stones. *See also* Yellow: Yellow Mountain Saxifrage; Purple: Purple Saxifrage; White: Mossy, Paniculate, Starry and Thick-leaved Saxifrage.

Verticillate Lousewort

Pedicularis verticillata – Pédiculaire verticillée – Quirlblättriges Läusekraut – Pedicolare a foglie verticillate

Emerging from dense undergrowth in woodland are these longish stalks topped with groups of pink-purplish flowers with a three-lobed lower lip. It also flowers on damp pastures in June–August up to 3100m. The name *Pedicularis* comes from the old, questionable belief that these plants gave livestock lice; however, there is no doubt that some species do host colonies of aphids. *See also* Yellow: Crested and Hacquet's Lousewort; Purple: Beaked Lousewort.

Aaron's Rod, Great Mullein

Verbascum thapsus – Molène thapsus –
Kleinblütige Königskerze – Verbasco tasso-barbasso

The spectacular robust spikes that reach 2m in height are plastered with small yellow flowers. Oblong silvery-grey furry leaves grow on the lower stalk. Widespread, it grows on dry stony terrain up to 1900m altitude and flowers June–September. The evocative common name refers to the staff carried by Moses' brother, which sprouted buds and blossoms in front of Pharaoh as proof of his God's power. *Verbascum* derives from 'beard' relating to the plant's furry aspect. In antiquity the pole-like stalk was used as a torch and its leaves as a wick, and also as a herbal remedy for coughs and skin problems. *See also* Dark Mullein.

Alpine Cabbage

Brassica repanda – Chou recourvé –
Ausgebreiter Kohl – Cavolo ricurvo

The plant has light yellow flowers with reddish stalks and small lance-like leaves with faint toothing. It forms attractive tufts on stony terrain. *Brassica* is derived from the Greek for 'I eat', denoting that the plant is edible – as reflected in all the foreign language names. It flowers May–August up to 2500m altitude in the western Alps.

Alpine Laburnam

Laburnam alpinum – Aubours des Alpes –
Alpen-Goldregen – Maggiociondolo alpino

Very aptly named 'golden rain' in the German, this small tree is hung with bunches of delicate pale yellow blooms as early as May and continuing through to July. It grows in woods across the Alps except for the central and north-eastern parts, up to 2000m altitude.

Arnica

Arnica montana – Arnica des montagnes – Arnika – Arnica

Single dishevelled yellow flowerheads with a light scent sit on the top of a long slender stalk as tall as 50cm. Oblong, untoothed leaves are positioned in perfectly opposite pairs on the lower stalk – these are key in telling it apart from the almost identical Leopardsbanes, whose leaves are alternate. Arnica is renowned for its medicinal properties such as an ointment for treating joint pains. The name may derive from the Greek for 'sneeze'; the leaves were used as snuff and were also smoked in northern Europe. Common across the Alps, it is found up to 2900m altitude and flowers June–August.

Bear's-ear

Primula auricula – Primevère auricle – Flühblümchen –
Primula orecchia d'orso

Quite a show-off, this unmistakable vibrant yellow primrose with dense clusters of flowers stands out clearly on bare rock surfaces, where its roots are firmly anchored in crannies; however, it also favours damp meadows. It sports large rounded fleshy leaves, often toothed. Blooms appear May–July up to 2900m altitude across all the Alps with a gap in the south. *See also* Oxlip and Primrose; Red: Bird's-eye and Stinking Primrose; Purple: Marginate Primrose.

Biting Stonecrop, Wallpepper

Sedum acre – Poivre de muraille – Scharfer Mauerpfeffer – Sedo acre

Veritable carpets of these vivid yellow ground-hugging succulents can be admired on dry stony terrain and old walls where sunshine is guaranteed. The tiny star-shaped flowers have prominent stamens and stand on short, pale red tinged fleshy stalks studded with tiny blunt oval-cylindrical leaves. It is evergreen and flowers June–August as high as 2300m altitude.

As Stonecrops are commonly found on walls and roofs, they were popularly believed to protect houses from lightning strikes and fires. The genus name derives from 'settle' as the leaves reportedly bring relief for wounds. *See also* Creamish Stonecrop; Red: Caucasian Stonecrop; White: Thick-leaved Stonecrop.

Buckler Mustard

Biscutella laevigata – Lunetière lisse –
Gewöhnliches Brillenschötchen –
Biscutella levigata

These sprays of small lemon yellow
flowers on long branched stems can
be seen in meadows and stony terrain. *Biscutella* refers to the double
shield-like seed pods, likened to read-
ing glasses by the French and German
names; while *laevigata* means 'pol-
ished'. It flowers June–August up to
2800m altitude across the Alps. *See
also* Coincya.

Carnic Lily

Lilium carniolicum – Lis de Carniole – Krainer Lilie –
Giglio della Carnia

It's a rare treat to come across one of these strikingly beautiful orange lilies
as they are found exclusively across the south-eastern Alps. They flower
May–August in meadows and
clearings up to 2300m altitude.
The petals of the large turk's cap
head are peppered with dark
spots – unlike the Lesser Turk's
Cap Lily that has just a few. The
leaves also dif-
fer: the Carnic
Lily has alternate,
oblong lance-
shaped leaves up
the stem, in con-
trast to the grass-
like leaves of the
other. *See also* Lesser Turk's Cap
Lily; Red: Martagon Lily.

Coincya

Coincya richeri – Coincye de Richer –
Richers Lacksenf – Senape di Richer

Also classified as a *Brassica* or as
Rhynchosinapis richeri, this has
bright rounded clusters of yellow mustard-coloured flowers on
multi-branched stalks with toothed
leaves a bit like a dandelion's. Both
parts of the plant name are dedicated to French botanists: the first
hailed from the 1800s, while the
second founded the Montpellier
botanical garden in the 1600s.
Limited to the western Alps, it
flowers June–August on rocky and
grassy terrain up to 2500m altitude. *See also* Buckler Mustard.

Coltsfoot

Tussilago farfara – Tussilage farfara – Huflattich – Tussilagine comune

One of the very first to appear after the end of winter (like crocuses), these
bright yellow flowers have short rays, scaly stalks and little in the way of
leaves – these appear at a
later date and, with a little
stretch of the imagination,
resemble a horseshoe. The
plant has traditionaly been
used in herbal medicine
for treating chest conges-
tion, and the name comes
from the Latin for 'gener-
ate coughing'. It is found
widely in woods and clearings up to 2800m altitude
and flowers February–May.

Common Cow-wheat

Melampyrum pratense – Mélampyre des prés –
Wiesen-Wachtelweizen – Melampiro dei prati

Rows or clusters of flimsy open-mouthed tube flowers that are yellow-white, sometimes tinged light purple, are attached to a spiky stalk that grows as tall as 50cm, and are accompanied by spear-like leaves tinged with a shade of red-brown, The main name means 'black wheat' as it was believed to turn flour black and toxic if ground together with the wheat; the tag is 'meadow'. The plant's present-day habitat is open woods and clearings up to 2500m altitude. It flowers June–October.

Creamish Stonecrop

Sedum ochroleuceum – Orpin des montagnes –
Gewöhnlicher Berg-Mauerpfeffer – Sedo montano

A tallish stonecrop, this one can reach 30cm. A single stem carries a well-

crammed cluster of yellow pointy star blooms that remain upright. Small pointed fleshy leaves are arranged diagonally down the stem, which may be red tinged; it can be confused with Yellow Mountain Saxifrage. It grows in patches on stony terrain and banks up to 2300m altitude across the western and central Alps, and flowers June–July. *See also* Biting Stonecrop; Red: Caucasian Stonecrop; White: Thick-leaved Stonecrop.

Creeping Avens

Geum reptans – Benoîte rampante –
Kriechende Berg-Nelkenwurz – Cariofillata strisciante

This is an eye-catching golden bloom that appears in dwarf bouquets or straggling spreads on moraines and broken rocky terrain. A single flower with notched petals and yellow stamens occupies a single stalk, growing close to the ground and surrounded by roundish multi-lobed leaves and runners. *Geum* is a reference to its scent as an essential oil can be extracted from its roots, while *reptans* means 'creep'. It flowers July–August up to 2800m altitude.

Crested Lousewort, Tufted Lousewort

Pedicularis comosa – Pédiculaire chevelue –
Schopfiges Läusekraut – Pedicolare chiomata

Pale lemon hooded flowers and feathery leaves all up its thick spiky stem distinguish this Lousewort. An inhabitant of meadows and stony slopes, it flowers June–August in the western and southern Alps up to 2300m altitude. The name *Pedicularis* derives from the questionable belief that these plants gave livestock lice; however, there is no doubt that some species host colonies of aphids. *See also* Hacquet's Lousewort; Red: Verticillate Lousewort; Purple: Beaked Lousewort.

Dark Mullein

Verbascum nigrum – Molène noire – Dunkle Königskerze – Verbasco nero

This attractive wide-spread Mullein can reach 1m in height and has a branched spike. It bears small yellow flowers with brilliant purple stamens that are furry and orange tipped, while the bright green leaves are pointed and spear-shaped. It flowers June–September on dry open terrain up to 1800m altitude. *See also* Aaron's Rod.

Dwarf Hawkweed

Hieracium humile – Épervière peu élevée – Niedriges Habichtskraut – Sparviere lacerato

Hardy clumps of golden flowers with blunt petals sprout almost miraculously out of stony terrain and rock surfaces. Its dark green elongated leaves are deeply toothed. Found extensively across the Alps, it flowers June–August on rocky terrain up to 2500m altitude. The name is derived from 'Hierax' or hawk, as it was commonly held that the birds made use of the plant's sap to improve their eyesight. *See also* Mouse-ear Hawkweed and Woolly Hawkweed.

Elder-flowered Orchid

Dactylorhiza sambucina – Orchis à odeur de sureau –
Holunder-Knabenkraut – Orchidea sambucina

Delicate pale yellow with tiny red-orange spots, this elegant orchid is found in damp meadows and clearings. Its elongated leaves are unspotted and it flowers March–July to 2100m altitude. Curiously, it also appears in a 'reverse' version – that is, purple-red with pale yellow spots. The main name means 'finger-shaped root', while the tag refers to the flower's elder scent. *See also* other orchids: Lady's Slipper; Red: Bee and Black Vanilla; Purple: Broad-leaved Marsh, Common Spotted and Heath Spotted; White: Burnt, Musk and Small White.

Genepi, Alpine Wormwood

Artemisia genipi – Genépi noir – Schwarze Edelraute – Genepì

This nondescript silvery dark-green woolly plant is especially aromatic,

and it is sought after for flavouring fiery spirits – the flowering tips are left to steep in alcohol (pickers need a permit). A type of Daisy, it has a composite flowerhead, with a soft yellow knob of tiny blooms. It grows up to 3100m altitude and flowers July–August. It probably took its name from Artemis, the Greek goddess of hunting, protector of the wood and of young girls – the plant was sacred to her – though it may also be a tribute to the eponymous 4th-century BC botanist, medical researcher and Queen of ancient Persia.

Globeflower

Trollius europaeus – Trolle d'Europe – Europäische Trollblume –
Botton d'oro

Gorgeous glossy golden
spheres top straight stems with
spreading palm-like leaves. The
Globeflower is easily distinguished from Marsh Marigold
and Buttercup as the flower
stays mostly closed. Found in
large numbers in shady clearings and open slopes up to
2800m altitude across the Alps,
they create miniature woods of
green and yellow as they flower
May–July. The name is derived
from the ancient German for
'globe'.

Golden Cinquefoil

Potentilla aurea – Potentille dorée – Gold-Fingerkraut –
Potentilla dorata

These pretty golden blooms have five notched petals. The *Potentilla*
label is a reference to the 'potence' of some species as a tonic and astringent,
while *aurea* comes from the Latin for 'gold'. A hairy plant with palmate

leaves of usually five leaflets, it
colonises rocky and grassy places
and forms eye-catching mats. It
is easily confused with Creeping
Avens, another prostrate plant
with bright yellow flowers; however, the difference lies in the leaf
shape. It flowers June–September
up to 2600m altitude. *See also*
Red: Pink Cinquefoil and White:
Lax Potentilla.

Goldenrod

Solidago virgaurea – Solidage verge d'or – Gewöhnliche Goldrute – Verga d'oro comune

This rather scruffy plant sports rich yellow flowers that are short-rayed, and has tall multi-branched stalks thick with buds and spear-like leaves. One of the few alpine flowers that can be still be admired in autumn – it flowers July–October – it grows in abundance in meadows and woods as high as 2800m altitude in all the alpine regions.

Great Yellow Gentian

Gentiana lutea – Gentiane jaune – Gelber Enzian – Genziana maggiore

You wouldn't single this out as a typical gentian. Masses of open yellow blooms with pointed petals (unlike the similar Spotted Gentian) are set at intervals on colossal stalks towering to 120cm from a large-leaved base. But this is the best known family member for its medicinal properties – it is used in the treatment of malarial fever. The name is a tribute to the 2nd-century BC Illyrian king Gentius who first discovered its virtues; he treated his troops with it against the plague. Nowadays Italians use the bitter root to flavour the fiery spirit grappa. It flowers June–August on meadows up to 2500m altitude across the Alps. It can be confused with poisonous White False Helleborine prior to flowering. *See also* Gentians: Spotted; Blue: Bladder, Clusius's, Cross, Fringed, Spring and Willow-leaved; Purple: Chiltern.

Grey Alpine Groundsel, Hoary Groundsel

Senecio incanus – Séneçon blanchâtre –
Graues Greiskraut – Senecio biancheggiante

This plant has composite flowers of a rich golden hue. Its stems and leaves can be either green or silvery grey, while the elongated leaves are pinnate. It grows on stony ground up to 3500m altitude and flowers July–September. A number of different subspecies are found across the Alps. The name comes from the Latin 'old', a reference to the show of fluff the plant produces with its seeds. *See also* Pinnate-leaved Ragwort.

Hacquet's Lousewort

Pedicularis hacquetii – Pédiculaire de Hacquet –
Hacquets Läusekraut – Pedicolare di Hacquet

The tall, partly parasitic plant bears copious pale yellow flowers and has straggly fern-like leaves. It was named after 18th century Austrian botanist Belsazar de la Motte Hacquet who travelled extensively through the Hapsburg Empire and wrote a treatise on the flora of Carniola. It flowers July–August up to 1700m altitude in woods in the southeast Alps. *See also* Crested Lousewort; Red: Verticillate Lousewort; Purple: Beaked Lousewort.

Heart-leaved Leopardsbane

Doronicum columnae – Doronic de Colonna –
Herzblättrige Gemswurz – Doronico di Colonna

Splendid clumps of this rich yellow member of the Daisy family brighten bare rocky terrain across the eastern Alps. It is easily distinguished from the more common Large-flowered Leopardsbane by its heart-shaped leaves, which are also veined and toothed. Stems up to 60cm tall carry single upright flowerheads. It flowers May–August up to 2300m altitude. The tag recalls the 16th-century Neapolitan Fabio Colonna, the first to use copper engravings to illustrate plants.

Horseshoe Vetch

Hippocrepis comosa – Hippocrépide à toupet – Hufeisenklee –
Sferracavallo comune

This plant forms thick mats of bright yellow flowers with green pinnate leaves. On short stalks radiating out in a crown formation, the flowers are typical of the Pea family, with a sort of hood and large lower lip. The twisted flattened seed pods separate into sections shaped like horseshoes, hence the name. It flowers April–August in both meadows and stony places up to 2800m altitude.

Imperforate St John's Wort

Hypericum maculatum – Millepertuis maculé –
Geflecktes Johanniskraut – Iperico macchiato

Attractive clusters of warm golden
flowers sport showy stamens and five
petals with tiny dark reddish dots and
streaks. This staining, which earned
it the tag *maculatum*, is caused by a
latex, dubbed the blood of John the
Baptist. Pairs of oval veined leaves
sprout off the orangey stalks. It flowers July–August in damp meadows and
edges of woods up to 2700m altitude,
over all but the far southern Alps. *See
also* Yellow Coris. St John's Wort comes
in many forms and is used extensively

in herbal medicine. The Latin name may derive from 'above the image' as
it was often placed over sacred icons. Until recently girls across Europe
would hang it in their bedroom on St John's night (23 June) and if it hadn't
wilted by morning, it meant they would find a husband!

Kidney-vetch

Anthyllis vulneraria – Anthyllide vulnéraire – Echter Wundklee –
Vulneraria comune

A member of the Pea family, as suggested by the appearance of the flowers,
this has elongated golden yellow flowers bunched together, with reddish-
brown sepals and stalks. *Anthyllis* comes from 'furry flower' whereas the tag

refers to the plant's capacity to
heal wounds. In medieval times
it was prized for protecting people and livestock alike from the
'evil eye'. There is a range of
subspecies and variations of this
plant. It flowers May–September
on rocky places and dry meadows as high as 3000m altitude.

Lady's Slipper Orchid

Cypripedium calceolus – Sabot de Vénus –
Frauenschuh – Pianella della Madonna

In a class all its own, this unmistakable spectacular orchid has slim maroon petals around a swollen slipper-shaped receptacle that is shiny yellow, and acts as a trap for insects. A profusion of large oblong veined leaves accompany the stalk. Found in clearings and near streams up to 2000m altitude, it flowers from May–July, and is increasingly rare – and protected. While 'pedium' is a reference to a sandal or footwear, the plant was principally named after the beautiful goddess Venus who was also known as Cypris, the Lady of Cyprus. Her name has survived in the French version, but curiously became 'our Lady' in Italian and in German too. *See also* other orchids: Elder-flowered; Red: Bee and Black Vanilla; Purple: Broad-leaved Marsh, Common Spotted and Heath Spotted; white: Burnt, Musk and Small White.

Large-flowered Leopardsbane

Doronicum grandiflorum – Doronic à grandes fleurs –
Grossblütige Gemswurz – Doronico a fiori grandi

Distributed extensively across the Alps on a variety of stony terrain, the marvellous sunshine-coloured flower owes its species name to the Arabic *dourondj*, referring to a plant that was either poisonous or of use in medicine. Its flowerheads are solitary, while the broad light grey-green leaves are hairy, toothed, veined and oval, in contrast to the less common Heart-leaved Leopardsbane. It grows quite tall, to a maximum of 40cm, and flowers July–August up to 2900m altitude.

Lesser Turk's Cap Lily, Red Lily

Lilium pomponium – Lis turban – Pompone-Lilie – Giglio pomponio

A rare red-orange lily with a surprisingly unpleasant odour, this grows only in the far south of the Alps, in geographical contrast to the very similar Carnic Lily that hails from the south-eastern Alps. The two can be distinguished by their leaves – in this case narrow blades that crowd the stalk – and by the light scattering of dark spots on the flower, contrasting with the many spots of the Carnic Lily. It flowers May–July on rocky places only as high as 1100m altitude. *See also* Carnic Lily and Red: Martagon Lily.

Light Yellow Broomrape

Orobanche lutea – Orobanche jaune – Gelbe Sommerwurz – Orobanche gialla

The name comes from the Greek for 'strangle legume' as this curious plant is a parasite, though it undeniably resembles an orchid. An upright stalk with inconspicuous scale-like leaves bears the tubular flowers. This pale yellow species is found across most of the central-eastern Alps in meadows up to 1500m altitude, flowering June–July. *See also* Red: Slender Broomrape.

Marsh Marigold, Kingcup

Caltha palustris – Caltha des marais –
Sumpf-Dotterblume – Calta palustre

Attractive shiny bunches of buttercup-like flowers on fleshy stalks are adorned with heart-shaped leaves that have serrated edges. They form colourful mats along streams, wet pastures and in marshes across the Alps up to 2500m altitude, and flower March–June. Named after the Greek for 'basket', the flower cups spread wide open, unlike the Globeflower which remains closed. In dried form, they can reportedly be used as a dye.

Mountain Pansy

Viola lutea – Pensée jaune –
Gelbes Alpen-Stiefmütterchen – Viola gialla

This unusually pretty pansy has distinctive dark markings in the centre and a broad lower lip. As well as yellow it also appears in violet or two-toned yellow-violet. It flowers June–August up to 2000m altitude on grassy and rocky places in parts of the eastern Alps.

Mouse-ear Hawkweed

Hieracium pilosella – Épervière pilosella –
Langhaariges Habichtskraut – Sparviere pelosetto

Single flowers of lemon yellow
with blunt petals, red-striped
underneath, sit atop a hairy
stem accompanied by furry
short elliptical leaves. The
plant's medicinal properties
were recognised back in medieval times as an anti-inflammatory and much else, though
nowadays it is considered a
weed. It flowers May–October
on grassy terrain and woods
as high as 3000m altitude. *See
also* Dwarf Hawkweed and
Woolly Hawkweed.

Orange Lily, Fire Lily

Lilium bulbiferum – Lis à bulbilles –
Brutknöllchentragende Feuerlilie – Giglio di San Giovanni

This is a brilliant, open-flow-
ered upright lily with splashes
of bright orange-red. The Latin
attribute *bulbiferum*, 'bearing
bulbs', refers to aerial bulbils
carried on the stem as an extra
guarantee of survival for the
plant. It flowers in meadows
and clearings May–July up to
1900m altitude in the central-
eastern Alps.

Oxlip

Primula elatior – Primevère élevée –
Wald-Schlüsselblume – Primula maggiore

Nodding pale yellow tube flowers hang in dense clusters from
one side of stems that grow as
tall as 30cm. For some obscure
reason the English name derives
from the Old English for 'ox
dung'. Both the crinkly leaves
and roots have long been used
in folk medicine for their diu-
retic and antibacterial properties. It flowers February–June in
meadows and damp woods up to
2700m altitude. *See also* Bear's-
ear and Primrose; Red: Bird's-eye
and Stinking Primrose; Purple:
Marginate Primrose.

Pinnate-leaved Ragwort

Senecio abrotanifolius – Séneçon à feilles d'aurore –
Eberreisblättriges Greiskraut – Senecio abrotanino

The bright orange-yellow
flower is reminiscent of
a scruffy daisy, and the
branched fleshy stalks are
thick with fern -like leaves.
Found on stony slopes up to
2700m altitude across all but
the eastern Alps, it flowers
July–September. *See also* Grey
Alpine Groundsel.

Primrose

Primula vulgaris – Primevère sans tige –
Schaftlose Schlüsselblume – Primula comune

Pretty lemon yellow flowers surrounded by basal felty veined leaves brighten wintery woods and scrubland. The term *Primula* was coined for this flower to denote its early spring flowering, and it symbolises youth. According to popular tradition it grew in the very place where St Peter dropped his keys, as confirmed by the German name. It blooms February–May up to 1500m altitude. *See also* Bear's-ear and Oxlip; Red: Bird's-eye and Stinking Primrose; Purple: Marginate Primrose.

Rhaetian Poppy

Papaver rhaeticum – Pavot orangé –
Rätischer Alpen-Mohn – Papavero dorato

Typically encountered in clumps on limestone screes and gravelly stream beds, this bright sweetly-scented poppy has fluttering transparent petals that are surprisingly resistent to strong winds. The flower is golden yellow and often tinged orange-red; rare examples are white – not to be confused with the Julian Poppy. The tag refers to the ancient Roman province of Rhaetia in the southern Alps, though the poppy is common across the Alps, with the exception of the central regions. It blooms July–August up to 3000m altitude. *See also* White: Alpine Poppy.

Roseroot

Rhodiola rosea – Rhodiole rose – Rosenwurz – Rodiola rosea

Reminiscent of the Spurge family, the fleshy plant forms a dome with dense clusters of grey-green stalks that bear purple-brown tinged leaves all the way up, while the flowers heads are showy dense group-ings of yellowy-orange blos-soms. It flowers June–August on screes as well as in some meadows as high as 3000m altitude. In ancient times the root was administered to new-lyweds in the belief it would ensure healthy offspring. The main name derives from the Greek for 'rose', from the rose-like fragrance given off by the root, an idea reinforced by the tag.

Spotted Gentian

Gentiana punctata – Gentiane ponctuée – Tüpfel-Enzian – Genziana punteggiata

In contrast to the typical blue gentians, this is a largish plant (maximum 60cm). It is characterised by clusters of upright bell-shaped flowers that are pale yellow with purplish spots, unlike the Great Yellow Gentian which has pointed petals and no spots.

It flowers July–September on meadows up to 3050m altitude over all but the north-eastern and south-western corners of the Alps. See the Great Yellow Gentian for the story behind the name. *See also* Gentians: Blue: Bladder, Clusius's, Cross, Fringed, Spring and Willow-leaved; Purple: Chiltern.

Swiss Wallflower, Treacle Mustard

Erysimum helveticum – Érysimum rhétique – Schweizer Schöterich – Violaciocca retica

Eye-catching clumps of lemon yellow flowers provide marvellous splashes of colour on otherwise bare rock terrain. The flowers are in groups, each with four rounded overlapping petals encircling yellow stamens. A low grower, it has small dark green leaves that are lance-shaped and may be toothed. It is found up to 3100m altitude across most of the Alps except for the far east, flowering June–August.

Tofield's Asphodel

Tofieldia calyculata – Tofieldie à calicule – Gewöhnliche Simsenlilie – Tofieldia comune

Minuscule lemon yellow flowers in oblong clusters at the top of pale green stalks make this plant look a bit like an orchid. Flat spear-like leaves grow from the base. It is found in marshes, damp rocks and meadows to 2500m altitude and flowers June–September. While widespread, it is neither common nor eye-catching, so tends to be ignored in favour of more spectacular plants. It is named after the 18th-century English botanist Thomas Tofield.

Woolly Hawkweed

Hieracium lanatum – Épervière tomenteuse –
Filziges Habichtskraut – Sparviere tomentosa

Eye-catching wavy leaves, which are silvery felted and woolly, belong to huge clumped plants that thrive on dry rocky grassland. The pale yellow flowers have blunt tips and come in crammed clusters. It flowers May–July to 2100m altitude in the western Alps. *See also* Dwarf Hawkweed and Mouse-ear Hawkweed.

Wulfen's House-leek

Sempervivum wulfenii – Joubarbe de Wulfen –
Wulfens Hauswurz – Semprevivo di Wulfen

Another triffid-like evergreen succulent, this has a stocky, light green trunk crowned with star-shaped flowers of lemon yellow. The leaves form attractive rosettes on the ground and are bluish-green – unlike those of the dark green-reddish Large-flowered House-leek. Wulfen was an Austrian Jesuit and eminent botanist from the late 1700s. The plant flowers July–August on rocky terrain up to 2700m altitude across most of the central-eastern Alps. *See also* Red: Cobweb, Common and Mountain House-leek.

Yellow Bellflower

Campanula thyrsoides – Campanule en thyrse –
Gewöhnliche Strauss-Glockenblume – Campanula gialla

Lime green stamens protrude from light yellow tube flowers crowded together on spikes. Multitudes of long wavy leaves grow up the stems. While the name means 'small bell', the tag derives from the Greek for an ear of corn, referring to the shape of the flowerhead. It flowers July–September up to 2700m altitude across all but a southern slice of the Alps.

Yellow Coris, Heath-leaved St John's Wort

Hypericum coris – Millepertuis coris –
Nadel-Johanniskraut – Iperico coris

An uncommon type of St John's Wort, this grows exclusively in the far southern Alps along with a couple of patches in central regions. It has the trademark brilliant yellow flowers with long stamens but is distinguished by the shape of the leaves, which form bunches of short needles attached to the stem. It flowers June–July on rocky terrain exposed to sunshine up to 2000m altitude. *See also* Imperforate St John's Wort.

Yellow Day Lily

Hemerocallis lilio-asphodelus –
Hémérocalle jaune – Gelbe Taglilie – Emerocallide gialla

This strikingly pretty lily grows extensively across Russia and China where it is commonly eaten. In all likelihood it found refuge in the northern edges of the Alps during the last Ice Age, though nowadays it grows in the south-east regions. The name 'day lily' is apt as the blooms are short-lived. Unusually tall for a lily at 120cm, it flowers May–July in meadows and woods up to 1500m altitude.

Yellow Foxglove

Digitalis grandiflora – Digitale à grandes fleurs –
Grossblütiger Fingerhut – Digitale gialla maggiore

Widely distributed across the Alpine chain, this attractive plant owes its Latin name to the flowers which are shaped like fingers of a glove. They grow in dense groups up spikes with shiny green furry leaves. The 'fox' prefix in the English name may derive from the German botanist Fuchs or, more fancifully, 'folks' or 'fairies', as the little people dwelt in the bell-like flowers. A less common purple form also exists. Highly poisonous, the flower's toxin is diluted for use in heart medication. It flowers June–August on stony terrain and in woods up to 2000m altitude.

Yellow Mountain Saxifrage

Saxifraga aizoides – Saxifrage faux aïzoon –
Bach-Steinbrech – Sassifraga gialla

This colourful saxifrage has rounded yellow petals around a yellow centre or orange-red petals around a red centre, with protruding stamens. Several flowers share a single stalk with short fleshy, needle-like leaves. A low creeping plant, it is not unlike the Stonecrops (see Biting Stonecrop and Creamish Stonecrop). It flowers in damp stony places June–September up to 3150m altitude. *See also* Red: Two-flowered Saxifrage; Purple: Purple Saxifrage; White Mossy, Paniculate, Starry and Thick-leaved Saxifrage.

Yellow Ox-eye

Buphthalmum salicifolium – Buphtalme à feuilles de saule –
Weidenblättriges Rindsauge – Buftalmo con foglie di salice

This bright yellow daisy-like flower with short lance-like leaves off a long slender stem grows as tall as 60cm. The descriptive name literally means 'ox eye with willow-like leaves'. It flowers June–September in woods and damp stony terrain up to 2050m altitude.

Yellow Pasque Flower

Pulsatilla sulphurea – Pulsatille soufrée –
Gelbe Alpen-Küchenschelle – Anemone sulfurea

With delicate pale yellow flowers and dark green fern-like leaves, it can be found in meadows as high as 2700m altitude over all but the eastern Alps. The plant is hairy and poisonous and appears in springtime, often in the presence of snow – thus Pasque/Easter; it flowers April–August. Afterwards a dishevelled seed head takes over; this gave rise to the name 'to move', as the slightest breeze shakes it. *See also* Purple: Common Pasque Flower; White: Alpine Pasque Flower.

Yellow Wood Violet, Twin-flowered Yellow Violet

Viola biflora – Pensée à deux fleurs –
Gelbes Bergveilchen – Viola biflora

Twin rich yellow flowers share a single stem, though solitary examples can also be found. A typical violet shape, this flower has large paired upper lobes and a small lower lip with traces of dark brown markings. The large kidney-shaped leaves have a coating of fine hairs. It hugs the ground and forms large colourful clumps in shady woods and damp places as high as 3000m altitude all across the Alps. The flowering period is April–August.

Alpine Clematis

Clematis alpina – Clématite des Alpes – Alpenrebe – Clematide alpina

Bluish-violet drooping four-petalled flowers appear in tree branches as this tenaceous climbing creeper confuses its leaves with those of its hosts. Found in woods and meadows across the Alps except for patches in the central west, it flowers May–July up to 2900m altitude.

Alpine Sow-thistle

Cicerbita alpina – Cicerbite des Alpes – Alpen-Milchlattich – Cicerbita alpina

Spreads of tufted pale blue or mauve flowers with blunt edges sprout in large numbers from a stem bearing masses of large toothed leaves ending in a pointed triangle. Known as mountain lettuce in many countries, this plant was once eaten, despite its extremely bitter taste. It flowers June–August on meadows up to 2200m altitude.

Alpine Squill

Scilla bifolia – Scille à deux feuilles –
Zweiblättriger Blaustern – Scilla bifoglia

This pretty meadow dweller appears in early springtime (March–May) and grows from a bulb: the genus name means a sort of onion. Star-like flowers appear on branched stems accompanied by two long shiny leaves (hence *bifolia*) that emerge straight from the ground. It flowers around 1500m altitude across all the Alps except for a patch in the central north.

Alpine Wood Forget-me-not

Myosotis alpestris – Mysotis alpestre –
Alpen-Vergissmeinnicht – Nontiscordardime alpino

These pretty azure flowers with a yellow eye belong to a low-growing plant on stony terrain and in damp meadows. Variations in petal colour depend on soil acidity. The short hairy leaves gave the plant its name *Myosotis*, 'mouse ear'. However,
a medieval German story gave rise to the common name: a knight and his lady were strolling along the banks of a river when he bent over to gather a bunch of the eye-catching flowers. Alas, dragged down by the weight of his armour he slipped into the water, calling out to his beloved, 'Vergiss mein nicht', forget me not! It flowers June–August up to 2800m altitude; it is similar to the rarer dwarf King of the Alps which has tiny basal leaves.

Argentera Pansy

Viola argenteria – Pensée de l'Argentera –
Argentera-Stiefmütterchen – Viola dell'Argentera

Found exclusively in the Maritime Alps of France and Italy and named after their loftiest mountain, this tiny exquisite blue-lilac pansy sprouts on scree slopes and in impossible rock crannies. Spoon-shaped leaves accompany the pale blooms. It is found at altitudes up to 2700m and flowers June–August.

Bladder Gentian

Gentiana utriculosa – Gentiane à calice renflé –
Schlauch-Enzian – Genziana a calice rigonfio

This is easily recognisable by its unusually enlarged winged calyx that terminates in a small bright blue flower with a white centre. Each plant has several branches. It flowers May–August in marshy places and meadows up to 3000m altitude, everywhere but the far eastern and western Alps. It is similar to Spring Gentian. See the Great Yellow Gentian for the story behind the name. *See also* Gentians: Clusius's, Cross, Fringed, Spring and Willow-leaved; Yellow: Great Yellow and Spotted; Purple: Chiltern.

Bluish Paederota

Paederota bonarota – Véronique de Buonarota –
Buonarota-Ehrenpreis – Bonarota comune

Tufted blue-lilac blooms and shiny oval dark-green toothed leaves cascade from rock crannies on limestone up to 2600m altitude. This short plant is found across the eastern and south-eastern Alps and flowers July–August. The name apparently derives from Greek for 'opal' due to the colour, while the tag is a reference to a Florentine senator who was the patron of the 18th-century botanist Pier Antonio Micheli.

Clusius's Gentian

Gentiana clusii – Gentiane de Clusius – Clusius' Enzian –
Genziana di Clusius

A gorgeous, plump iridescent-blue trumpet-like gentian with dark spotting and streaking, each short stem supports a single flower, with rounded basal leaves. Widespread across all but the south-western Alps, it flowers March–August on grassy stony terrain up to 2800m altitude. It was named in honour of a 16th-century French pioneer in alpine flora study. See the Great Yellow Gentian for the story behind the genus name. *See also* Gentians: Bladder, Cross, Fringed, Spring and Willow-leaved; Yellow: Great Yellow and Spotted; Purple: Chiltern.

Common Monkshood

Aconitum napellus – Aconit napel – Blauer Eisenhut –
Aconito napello

This very attractive dark blue-violet flower flourishes around alpine farms and in damp meadows wherever the soil is rich in nitrogen, thanks to livestock. The flower resembles a helmet or a hood, and has a blackish centre. Bright green palmate spreading leaves grow most of the way up the stem, which reaches a maximum of 150cm. It is highly poisonous, earning it myriad nicknames: called 'vegetable arsenic' by Pliny, or 'devil's root'. The irritants can be absorbed through the skin so avoid handling! It was reportedly used in prehistoric times for killing wolves and foxes as well as poisoning spear tips for battle. It flowers June–August up to 2600m altitude. *See also* Variegated Monkshood.

Cross Gentian

Gentiana cruciata – Gentiane croisette – Kreuz-Enzian –
Genziana crociata

Light blue flowers with a purple outer coating peek out from the intersection of glossy veined pointed leaves at intervals down the stem. It is in fact the arrangement of the abundant leaves that give the plant its tag, and makes it unique amongst the gentians. See the Great Yellow Gentian for the explanation of the family name. It is found in meadows and rocky terrain up to 1600m altitude, and blooms June–August. *See also* Gentians: Bladder, Clusius's, Fringed, Spring and Willow-leaved; Yellow: Great Yellow and Spotted; Purple: Chiltern.

Einsel's Columbine

Aquilegia einseleana – Ancolie de Einsele –
Einseles Akelei – Aquilegia di Einsele

This exquisite columbine features a dark blue-violet nodding bonnet-like flower with straight spurs above feathery three-lobed leaves. It flowers June–July across parts of the central Alps as high as 1800m altitude and its habitat is open woods and stony terrain, usually limestone. The Latin name means 'eagle' as the flower's spur is said to resemble a talon. This variety was dedicated to Einsele, a Bavarian doctor and florist from the 1800s. *See also* Purple: Dark Columbine.

Fringed Gentian

Gentianella ciliata – Gentiane ciliée – Gefranster Enzian –
Genziana sfrangiata

Commonly found on the edge of woodland or on dry stony grassland up to 2200m altitude, this is one of the alpine flowers that can still be enjoyed in the autumn as it flowers August–November. Its longish dull blue-purple petals are often pointed and have noticeably fringed edges – thus the *ciliata* tag. See the Great Yellow Gentian for the explanation of the family name. *See also* Gentians: Bladder, Clusius's, Cross, Spring and Willow-leaved; Yellow: Great Yellow and Spotted; Purple: Chiltern.

Grape-hyacinth

Muscari botryoides – Muscari botryoïde – Kleine Traubenhyazinthe – Muscari botrioide

Clusters of blue bulbous 'grapes', rimmed with white, droop from short fleshy stems. The leaves are grooved green slivers. Found in fields and woods in patches across the Alps, it flowers March–May up to 2000m altitude. It may have been named after the perfume musk due to a similar fragrance.

Hairy Bellflower

Campanula barbata – Bärtige Glockenblume – Campanule barbue – Campanula barbata

This pale blue bellflower is immediately identifiable due to the dense masses of fine white hairs that cover the flowers mostly inside but also outside. These come in nodding bunches on longish stalks, and oblong leaves with wavy edges sprout from the base. The plant grows widely on meadows and stony terrain across the Alps up to 3000m altitude, and flowers June–August. *See also* Bellflowers Yellow: Yellow, Blue: Mont Cenis, Moretti's, Spiked, Purple: Clustered, Spreading.

Harebell

Campanula rotundifolia – Campanule à feuilles rondes –
Rundblättrige Glockenblume – Campanula a foglie rotonde

This delicate nodding light blue flower grows widely and with many variant forms all across the Alps. Paper-thin bells balance on long slender stems with the odd narrow lance-shaped leaf; however, the base is crowded with roundish leaves. It is found on grassland, open wood and rocky terrain up to 2200m altitude and flowers May–October.

Hepatica, Liver Flower

Hepatica nobilis – Hépatique à trois lobes –
Leberblümchen – Erba trinità

Posies of these exceptionally attractive pastel blue or pink-lilac flowers are commonly encountered in the woods in springtime, standing out against dried brown leaves on the ground. It generally has seven petals in a saucer arrangement, and sports prominent white stamens. The name came from the Greek 'liver' due to the shape of its leaves, and it was reportedly used to treat liver complaints. Its habitat includes rocky and grassy places up to 2200m altitude and it flowers March–May.

Horned Rampion

Phyteuma scheuchzeri – Raiponce de Colonna – Horn-Rapunzel – Raponzolo di Colonna

This rather straggly solitary deep blue flower is typical of the Rampion family with a long protruding stigma and tube-like flower segments with twirly bits at the tip. Lance-like leaves alternate along the stalk. It flowers June–August on rocky slopes to 2600m, mostly in the southern Alps. Rampions were attributed with aphrodisiac properties in ancient times. This one was named after an 18th-century Swiss botanist. *See also* Rosette-leaved and Scorzonera-leaved Rampion; Purple: Dark Rampion.

King of the Alps

Eritrichium nanum – Éritriche nain – Himmelsherold – Eritrichio nano

Forming a brilliant blue hairy cushion found in crannies and on consolidated screes, this plant clings to the rock surface. Like the Forget-me-nots it has a yellow eye, but can be distinguished by its dwarf stature and tiny oblong leaves, gathered at the base. It is found up as high as 3600m altitude across all but the northern and western-most fringes of the Alps, flowering July–August. The name refers to the plant's dense silky hairs, while the tag means 'dwarf'.

Larkspur, Delphinium

Delphinium dubium – Dauphinelle douteuse –
Zweifelhafter Rittersporn – Speronella alpina

Charming nodding sky blue flowers with dark centres adorn this bushy plant that forms large clumps. The leaves are palmate with deep cuts. It grows on meadows and stony terrain and flowers June–August. It is found up to 2300m across the western and central-south Alps. It is poisonous, as are the look-alike Monkshoods.

Leafless-stemmed Globularia, Naked-stalked Globe-daisy

Globularia nudicaulis – Globulaire è tige nue –
Nacktstänglige Kugelblume – Globularia a fusto nudo

These pretty pale blue flowerheads with a straggly tangle of petals and stamens give the impression of being woolly. The dark green leaves are folded inwards, like a scoop. A mat-forming plant, it grows on rock surfaces and open woods up to 2700m altitude throughout the Alps except for pockets in the far south, and flowers July–September.

Meadow Clary

Salvia pratensis – Sauge des prés – Gewöhnliche Wiesen-Salbei – Salvia dei prati

Bright blue-purple flowers adorn long spikes in grassland and rich meadows up to 1900m altitude. The large oval base leaves are furry and veined, while smaller leaves punctuate the stalk. It flowers May–August. The name classifies it as a type of sage, an aromatic herb, while the tag refers to its propensity to grow in meadows.

Mont Cenis Bellflower

Campanula cenisia – Campanule du Mont Cenis – Mont-Cenis-Glockenblume – Campanula del Moncenisio

Delicate light blue waxy blooms of five petals extend over on rock faces forming hardy mats with tiny bluish leaves. It flowers July–September on screes and moraines up to 3100m altitude in the central-western Alps where it is endemic. The first specimen to be identified probably came from Mont Cenis in the French Alps.

Moretti's Bellflower

Campanula morettiana – Campanule de Moretti –
Dolomiten-Glockenblume – Campanula di Moretti

Rock overhangs and cran-
nies up to 2300m altitude are
festooned with blue-purple
clumps of eye-catching bellflowers, a savvy choice of
habitat that ensures protection from the elements. Tiny
notched shield-shaped leaves
shelter further back. Flowering
July–August, the plant grows
in abundance in the Italian
Dolomites and eastern Alps,
where it is endemic. Moretti
was an Italian botanist from
the early 1800s.

Mountain Cornflower, Perennial Cornflower

Centaurea montana – Centaurée des montagnes –
Berg-Flockenblume – Centaurea montana

The curious flower is made up
of soft blue feathers around
a fluffy purple centre, atop a
round knob of hard woody
scales. It grows on meadows
and open woodland to 2100m
altitude in all but the central-
south Alps, and flowers May–
August. The plant is a symbol
of intelligence, and the name
may be homage to the legendary centaur Chiron who used it
as a medicine. *See also* Purple:
Single-flowered Knapweed.

Mountain Flax, Perennial Flax

Linum alpinum – Lin des Alpes – Alpen-Lein – Lino celeste

Branched bunches of pale blue five-petalled blooms with darker faint veining come on a slender stem, with modest narrow leaves. Found in grassy places, it blooms June–August up to 1800m altitude, and is widespread except for the central-northern Alps. The oil extracted from its seeds is used in cosmetics.

Pyramidal Bugle

Ajuga pyramidalis – Bugle pyramidale – Pyramiden-Günsel – Bugola piramidale

This striking plant stands out among the green grass in damp meadows and woods, flowering April–September up to 2000m altitude. Its sky blue or purplish flowers with white stripes peep out from closely packed layers of hairy oval leaves that are purplish-green and alternate down the stem. The strange genus name comes from the Latin for 'without a yoke', referring to the shape of the flower which lacks an upper lip. It resembles purple Alpine Bartsia.

Queen of the Alps, Alpine Eryngo

Eryngium alpinum – Panicaut des Alpes – Alpen-Mannstreu –
Eringio delle Alpi

A remarkably beautiful flower that is both rare and endangered, this fantastic giant thistle can grow as tall as a metre. A tight cluster of tiny blooms form a cylindrical flowerhead with a ruff of metallic blue-lilac spikes, and the colouring often continues through the upper plant. It flowers July–September up to 2500m altitude in the north-western and south-eastern Alps. The name purportedly derives from Greek terms for 'hedgehog' and 'defence', referring to the plant's capacity to avoid becoming a meal for a herbivore.

Rock Speedwell

Veronica fruticans – Véronique buissonnante – Felsen-Ehrenpreis –
Veronica fruticosa

Iridescent blue petals around a distinctive red and white centre set this beauty aside from other Speedwells.

The creeping plant has small oval leaves, and is found on stony terrain and grassland as high as 3000m altitude. It flowers May–August, often starting close to Easter week, which is one explanation for the genus name as Saint Veronica was a pious woman of Jerusalem who, according to tradition, gave Christ her veil to wipe away his sweat en route to Golgotha.

Rosette-leaved Rampion

Phyteuma globulariifolium – Raiponce è feuilles de globulaire –
Armblütige Rapunzel – Raponzolo con foglie di globularia

The small ground-hugging plant with a showy deep blue flower resembles a spider with thick outstretched legs. The short straight leaves have turned-in edges. It flowers on rocks and scree July–September across most of the central and eastern Alps up to 3000m altitude. *See also* Horned and Scorzonera-leaved Rampion and Purple: Dark Rampion.

Scorzonera-leaved Rampion

Phyteuma scorzonerifolium – Raiponce è feuilles de scorzonère –
Schwarzwurzelblättrige Rapunzel – Raponzolo con foglie di scorzonera

A single stem holds each light blue flowering head which is cylindrical and spear-headed, and can be rather scruffy. Thin faintly toothed lance-like leaves are further down the stem. It flowers July–August in open woods and meadows to 2200m altitude in the southern Alps. *See also* Horned and Rosette-leaved Rampion and Purple: Dark Rampion.

Spiked Bellflower

Campanula spicata – Campanule en épi –
Ährige Glockenblume – Campanula spigata

The handsome tall spiked plant is crowded with elongated bell-shaped blue-lilac flowers that grow upwards. It is found up to 2400m altitude across most of the Alpine chain, with the exception of the northern edges and the north-west Alps, and flowers July–August on meadows and stony places.

Spring Gentian

Gentiana verna – Gentiane printanière – Frühlings-Enzian –
Genziana primaverile

The very first gentian of the year to bloom, it boasts tiny five-petalled solitary blooms with a white centre. The petal colour can vary from pale to brilliant deep blue. The lance-shaped leaves are bright green and clustered around the base. A key distinguishing feature is the calyx with narrow wings. It is found on meadows and rocky terrain as high as 3000m altitude, and flowers March–July. See Great Yellow Gentian for the story behind the name. *See also* Gentians: Bladder, Clusius's, Cross, Fringed and Willow-leaved; Yellow: Great Yellow and Spotted; Purple: Chiltern.

Variegated Monkshood

Aconitum variegatum – Aconit panaché –
Gewöhnlicher Bunter Eisenhut – Aconito screziato

Less common and paler than Common Monkshood, this has a light blue helmet flower that is streaked with white and has prominent veining. It can grow as tall as 150cm, and is found in damp meadows and near farms up to 2000m altitude. It flowers June–August and is sometimes confused with Larkspur.

Willow-leaved Gentian

Gentiana asclepiadea – Gentiane à feuilles d'aslépiade –
Schwalbenwurz-Enzian – Genziana asclepiade

An attractive member of the Gentian family, this can be admired well into autumn as it flowers August–October. Long bright blue trumpets streaked with white and purple appear in upright clusters on bushy plants that thrive in pasture and open woods up to 2200m altitude. Rows of pointed lance-like leaves are aligned along the stems. See Great Yellow Gentian for the story behind the name. The tag is homage to Asclepius, the Greek god of medicine and healing. *See also* Gentians: Bladder, Clusius's, Cross, Fringed and Spring; Yellow: Great Yellow and Spotted; Purple: Chiltern.

Adenostyles

Adenostyles alliariae – Adénostyle è feuilles d'alliaire –
Grauer Alpendost – Adenostile con foglie di alliaria

Large, bright green heart-shaped leaves that are veined and serrated accompany tight clusters of tiny tube flowers, dull lilac-pink in colour on multi-branched stems. The tall plant forms vast thickets alongside mountain streams and in damp rocky places up to 2700m altitude across the Alps, flowering June–September. *See also* White-leaved Adenostyles.

Alpine Bartsia

Bartsia alpina – Bartsie des Alpes – Alpenhelm –
Bartsia alpine

Unassuming but common, this plant is partly parasitic. The dark purple flowers are all but camouflaged by similarly coloured toothed paired leaves that are green lower down. It likes damp places and is found up to 2700m altitude, flowering June–August. Linnaeus named it after a valued medical friend of his who tragically lost his life in Dutch Guiana (now Suriname). It resembles Pyramidal Bugle.

Alpine Calamint

Acinos alpinus – Sarriette des Alpes –
Geschecktes Bohnenkraut – Santoreggia variegata

This ground-hugging creeper has tiny round leaves and violet tube flowers with a white centre and open lips. It lives on rock surfaces and scree as well as in meadows, and flowers June–September up to 2500m altitude. The main name derives from the Greek for 'basil' because of the resemblance of the leaves.

Alpine Skullcap

Scutellaria alpina – Scutellaire des Alpes –
Alpen-Helmkraut – Scutellaria delle Alpi

This shortish plant boasts rather scruffy, large lilac-white labiate flowers. The small veined leaves are oval, toothed and hairy. It flowers July–September on screes and grassy slopes up to 2500m altitude, mostly in the western Alps. The main name means 'small dish', refering to the shape of the calyx. In traditional Chinese medicine the plant has a long-standing reputation for boosting the immune system.

Alpine Snowbell

Soldanella alpina – Soldanelle des Alpes –
Gewöhnliches Alpenglöckchen – Soldanella alpina

Dainty purple-pink fringed flowers in clusters of 2–4 are supported by slender stems with rounded basal leaves. This is one of the first flowers out in spring, often pushing its way up through thawing snow. It flowers April–July up to 3000m altitude. Oddly, the genus may owe its name to the *solidus*, a Roman coin introduced by the Emperor Constantine, evidently of similar shape to the leaf. However, according to legend, the flower was a young girl who lived for spring and wasted away during winter.

Alpine Toadflax

Linaria alpina – Linaire des Alpes – Alpen-Leinkraut – Linaria alpina

Exquisite posies of snap-dragon-type flowers survive very nicely, firmly anchored to mobile terrain such as scree slopes across most of the Alps. Lilac flowerheads with a bright orange or, less common, white central lip sprout from grey-green leaf rosettes. It flowers June–September up to 3800m altitude.

Beaked Lousewort

Pedicularis rostratospicata – Pédiculaire à bec et en épi –
Schweizer Läusekraut – Pedicolare a spiga allungata

The spindly plant has two-toned dark purple-pink beaked flowers attached to a stem with small feathery pinnate leaves. It prefers open grassed terrain up to 2800m altitude in most of the eastern and central Alps, and flowers July–August. The main name derives from the old questionable belief that these plants gave livestock lice, whereas the tag means 'beaked'. *See also* Yellow: Crested and Hacquet's Lousewort; Red: Verticillate Lousewort.

Broad-leaved Marsh Orchid

Dactylorhizia majalis – Orchis à larges feuilles –
Breitblättriges Knabenkraut – Orchidea a foglie larghe

This deep mauve-pink orchid has a sturdy stalk and low spreading dark green leaves with large dark purple spots. It flowers May–July on damp meadows up to 2500m altitude. The main name means 'finger-shaped root'. *See also* Orchids: Common Spotted and Heath Spotted; Red: Bee and Black Vanilla; Yellow: Elder-flowered and Lady's Slipper; White: Burnt, Musk and Small White.

Chiltern Gentian, German Gentian

Gentianella germanica – Gentiane d'Allemagne –
Deutscher Enzian – Genzianella germanica

Upright lilac flowers comprise a dainty fringed centre surrounded by five pointed petals (the Field Gentian has four). Both the elongated calyx and the stems can be dark brown-green, especially at the end of the season. Found in meadows and stony terrain up to 2700m altitude all across the Alps except for patches in the south-east, it flowers June–October. See the Great Yellow Gentian for the story behind the name. *See also* Gentians: Yellow: Great Yellow and Spotted; Blue: Bladder, Clusius's, Cross, Fringed, Spring and Willow-leaved.

Clustered Bellflower

Campanula glomerata – Campanule agglomérée –
Gewöhnliche Knäuel-Glockenblume – Campanula agglomerata

Tall reddish stalks bear attractive clusters of deep purple-blue pointed five-petalled flowers with visible white anthers. Small oblong leaves are found at intervals down the stalk. Found widely in meadows and on the edges of woods up to 1700m altitude, it flowers June–September.

Common Butterwort

Pinguicula vulgaris – Grassette vulgaire –
Gewöhnliches Fettkraut – Pinguicola comune

The delicate beauty of this purple and white bloom belies its true nature as a devourer of insects. The main name is a derivation of Latin for greasy or fatty, due to the stickiness of its leaves which act as insect traps, like flypaper. It flowers May–July on damp terrain and rocks near watercourses up to 2300m altitude. *See also* White: Alpine Butterwort.

Common Lavender

Lavandula angustifolia – Lavande à feiulles étroites –
Echter Lavendel – Lavanda a foglie strette

Dense scented clusters of woolly lilac-blue flowers bloom at the tip of long stalks above small spear-like leaves. It flowers on sunny rocky ground June–August up to 1800m altitude in the far eastern Alps. Of many virtues, when fresh it keeps mosquitoes away and when dried, moths out of linen. The name derives from the Latin 'to wash', and the ancient Greeks and Romans bathed in the essence. However, the plant was reputedly bestowed its divine perfume when Mary hung baby Jesus' clothes on it to dry.

Common Pasque Flower

Pulsatilla vulgaris – Pulsatille vulgaire –
Gewöhnliche Küchenschelle – Anemone pulsatilla

The short hairy plant bears lovely blooms that vary from lilac to dark purple, with bright yellow anthers and a central purple spike. The flowers are initially erect but droop later. The plant is poisonous and flowers in springtime (March–May), often in the presence of snow. A dishevelled seed head takes over and explains the main name 'to move', as the slightest breeze shakes it. *See also* Yellow: Yellow Pasque Flower; White: Alpine Pasque Flower.

Common Spotted Orchid

Dactylorhiza fuchsii – Orchis tacheté –
Geflecktes Knabenkraut – Orchidea macchiata

A striking orchid with a showy head of purple-crimson, the flower comprises a large lobed lower lip with intricate loop markings and a small hood on a stem that is often tinged with purple. The long elliptical leaves always have dark spots. The main name means 'finger-shaped root'. It flowers May–August in meadows and clearings up to 2200m altitude. *See also* Orchids: Broad-leaved Marsh and Heath Spotted; Red: Bee and Black Vanilla; Yellow: Elder-flowered and Lady's Slipper; White: Burnt, Musk and Small White.

Dark Columbine

Aquilegia atrata – Ancolie noirâtre –
Schwarzviolette Akelei – Aquilegia nerastra

Found in limestone rock set-
tings and shady clearings,
this columbine has striking
dark purple-wine red flowers and protruding yellow
stamens. It flowers June–July
up to 2000m altitude across
the Alps except for pockets in
the far west. The main name
means 'eagle' as the flower's
spur resembles a talon; the
plant was once a symbol of
secret love. *See also* Blue:
Einsel's Columbine.

Dark Rampion

Phyteuma ovatum – Raiponce ovoïde –
Hallers Rapunzel – Raponzolo ovato

This blackish-violet spiky flower
sports twirly stigma and stands
atop a tall stem, with heart-shaped
leaves clustered around the lower
part. It flowers June–August in
meadows and woods up to 2400m
altitude across all but the eastern Alps. *See also* Blue: Horned,
Rosette-leaved and Scorzonera-
leaved Rampion.

Devil's Claw

Physoplexis comosa – Physoplexis chevelue – Schopfrapunzel – Raponzolo di roccia

Endemic to the south-eastern Alps, this dazzling flower is unusual. Its pale lilac-pinkish bulbous flowers have curly stigma and small oblong leaves that are bright green and toothed. It lives on vertical rock faces where its roots penetrate cracks in search of moisture, and flowers July–August up to 2000m altitude. The main name derives from 'swollen' and 'intricate', and the tag 'luxurious head of hair' – both referring in all probability to the flower shape.

Dusky Cranesbill, Mourning Widow

Geranium phaeum – Géranium brun – Brauner Storchschnabel – Geranio stellato

The vivid purple-vermilion or brown flowers come with a white centre and pronounced twirly stamens. The leaves are multi-lobed and pointed. It is found in damp meadows up to 2400m altitude across the Alps, and flowers June–August. *See also* Wood Cranesbill and Red: Rock and Silvery Cranesbill.

Great Meadow-rue, French Meadow-rue

Thalictrum aquilegifolium – Pigamon à feuilles d'ancolie –
Akeleiblättrige Wiesenraute – Pigamo con foglie di aquilegia

Delicate fluffy soft spiky petals form globes, and a lilac hue comes from the long stamens. The flowers are clustered together on long slender branching stalks with dark green pinnate leaves like those of the Columbine, which explains the Latin tag. It prefers damp meadows up to 2500m altitude and flowers May–July.

Heather, Ling

Calluna vulgaris – Callune vulgaire –
Heidekraut – Brugo

A common spreading shrubby plant with countless tiny purple bell-like flowers in rows on spiky twig-like stems covered with tiny dark green leaves. It colonises heaths and open woodland up to 2700m altitude and flowers July–November. The main name derives from the Greek 'to sweep' and some types are still used to make brushes.

Heath Spotted Orchid

Dactylorhiza maculata – Orchis tacheté –
Geflecktes Knabenkraut – Orchidea macchiata

The flowers of this particularly elegant orchid have delicate lilac markings with lines of dots against a white background. The main name means 'finger-shaped root' while the tag means 'spotted'. It is fairly common across the Alps up to 2200m altitude, and flowers May–July in heaths and bogs. *See also* Orchids: Broad-leaved Marsh and Common Spotted; Red: Bee and Black Vanilla; Yellow: Elder-flowered and Lady's Slipper; White: Burnt, Musk and Small White.

Long-spurred Pansy, Spurred Violet

Viola calcarata – Pensée éperonnée –
Langsporniges Stiefmütterchen – Viola speronata

This large-flowered violet-cum-pansy can be admired everywhere but the eastern Alps. Its bright purple flowers have a distinct yellow centre and a smaller lower lip, sometimes triangular in shape. It adorns rock surfaces and meadows up to 2400m and flowers May–August.

Marginate Primrose

Primula marginata – Primevère marginée –
Bestäubte Primel – Primula marginata

Apparently inhospitable places such as bare rock ledges and crevices and also screes in the southwestern Alps up to 2600m altitude are home to this eye-catching Primrose. Pastel lilac or bluish petals in bright bunches emerge from fleshy leaves that have deeply serrated edges. It flowers May–July. *See also* Red: Bird's-eye and Stinking Primrose; Yellow: Bear's-ear, Oxlip and Primrose.

Meadow Saffron, Autumn Crocus

Colchicum autumnale – Colchique d'automne –
Herbstzeitlose – Colchico autunnale

Also known as 'naked lady' because its flowers emerge 'unclothed' straight out of the ground in late summer, once the leaves have died off, it flowers August–October in shady meadows and open woods up to 2000m altitude. According to legend it was created inadvertently one day when Medea, daughter of the king of the ancient Georgian state of Colchis, was concocting a magic potion and spilled a drop on the ground. It is highly poisonous due to the colchicine, which has been used for treating rheumatism and gout since the time of the ancient Egyptians. Traditionally, even carrying a bulb in your pocket ensured protection from toothache, dysentery and the plague. *See also* White: White Crocus.

Mountain Kidney-vetch

Anthyllis montana – Anthyllide des montagnes –
Gewöhnlicher Berg-Wundklee – Antillide montana

These purple-crimson clover-like flowers are gathered into a rounded downy head. The plant creeps over limestone and other rocks forming a dense carpet with masses of grey pinnate leaves. It flowers May–July up to 2400m altitude in the far western Alps. The main name comes from the Greek for 'hairy flower'.

Mountain Milk-vetch

Oxytropis jacquinii – Oxytropis de Jacquin – Berg-Spitzkiel –
Astragalo di Jacquin

A sprawling plant with hairy green-grey pinnate leaves, it creeps over stony terrain up to 2900m altitude. The pretty purple-crimson tube flowers come in rounded bunches at the end of reddish stems and bloom June–August. It is also called Astragalus montanus, and was named after the 18th-century Baron Nicolaus Joseph von Jacquin, founder of the Viennese school of botany. It grows extensively across the Alps, except for the south-west.

Purple Saxifrage

Saxifraga oppositifolia – Saxifrage à feuilles opposées – Gegenblättriger Steinbrech – Sassifraga a foglie opposte

Barely centimetres off stony ground are woody pincushions of dull grey-green rosettes punctuated with mauve five-petalled flowers with a darkish centre. Widespread across the Alps as high as 3800m altitude, it flowers April–August. *See also* Red: Two-flowered Saxifrage; Yellow: Yellow Mountain Saxifrage; White: Grey, Mossy, Paniculate, Starry and Thick-leaved Saxifrages.

Round-leaved Pennycress

Thlaspi rotundifolium – Tabouret è feuilles rondes – Rundblättriges Täschelkraut – Tlaspi a foglie rotonde

A pioneer on mobile scree slopes, this plant forms eye-catching clumps

of honey-scented lilac or pinkish blooms, flowering May–September up to 3000m altitude. The main name comes from the Greek 'to squash', a reference to grinding the seeds of *Thlaspi* species to create a poultice; the green parts are rich in vitamin C and evidently can be eaten fresh.

Self-heal

Prunella vulgaris – Brunelle vulgaire –
Kleine Brunelle – Prunella comune

Modest hooded purple flowers sprout from heads rounded like pine cones. These emerge from a spreading bright green carpet of slightly hairy veined leaves. It grows in woods, dry meadows and stony ground up to 2400m altitude, flowering June–October. Self-heal is famous the world over for its extensive applications in traditional medicine as far back as 3rd-century BC China.

Single-flowered Knapweed

Centaurea nervosa – Centaurée nervée –
Federige Flockenblume–Centaurea nervosa

This attractive thistle-like plant is tagged *nervosa* presumably because of its dishevelled head of straggly purplish-red flowers. These sprout from a hairy bulbous nut. Toothed lance-like leaves are found all the way up the unbranched stem. It is widely distributed over all but the north-eastern Alps, and flowers July–August. The main name may be homage to the legendary centaur Chiron who used it in medicine. *See also* Blue: Mountain Cornflower.

Solid-tubered Corydalis, Bird-in-a-bush

Corydalis solida – Corydale à tubercule plein –
Fester Lerchensporn – Coridalide solida

In springtime woodland floors are covered with clumps of curious pale lilac clusters of long lipped tubes with a curving spur. This shape explains the name, from the Greek for 'crested lark'. It also has fern-like leaves and a long tuber. It flowers March–May in open woods and fields up to 2000m altitude everywhere but the northern Alps.

Spreading Bellflower

Campanula patula – Campanule étalée –
Gewöhnliche Wiesen-Glockenblume – Campanula a rami patenti

These attractive dainty bell-shaped blooms with five pointed petals come in vivid violet or blue-purple. Its stalks are especially thin and carry slender leaves with faint toothing. It can be found in grass and light woodland up to 2000m altitude everywhere except parts of the eastern and southern Alps, and flowers June–August. *See also* Bellflowers Yellow: Yellow, Blue: Bearded, Mont Cenis, Moretti's, Spiked, Purple: Clustered.

White-leaved Adenostyles

Adenostyles leucophylla – Adénostyle è feuilles blanches –
Filziger Alpendost – Adenostile a foglie bianche

The attractive pale woolly-leaved plant gives rise to low-lying silvery carpets across mountainsides. The flowers are small tubes of dull lilac-pink on multi-branched stems. It grows alongside mountain streams and in damp rocky places in the central-western Alps up to 3100m altitude, and flowers July–August. *See also* Adenostyles.

Wild Thyme

Thymus serpyllum – Thym précoce – Frühblühender Thymian –
Timo selvatico

A jumble of tiny bright green oval leaves and light purple flowers in crown-like clusters form compact matted carpets that creep across grass and rock surfaces. The plant, also known as *Thymus praecox*, flowers June–September up to 3000m altitude. Crushed underfoot, it fills the air with a delicious pungent scent as oil is released. The name derives from ancient Egyptian for 'perfume', and it was essential for embalming mummies. The plant also symbolised courage, and soldiers once bathed in thyme water.

Wood Cranesbill

Geranium sylvaticum – Géranium des forêts –
Wald-Storchschnabel – Geranio dei boschi

Purple flowers with rounded petals containing shades of red-pink and a whitish centre stand upright atop a tall slender stalk that also bears light green, cut palmate leaves. Widespread, it can be found as high as 2400m altitude in meadows and woods, as the name suggests. The flowering period is June–August. *See also* Dusky Cranesbill and Red: Rock and Silvery Cranesbill.

Woolly Thistle

Cirsium eriophorum – Cirse laineux –
Gewöhnliche Wollkopf-Kratzdistel – Cirsio lanoso

This tall showy thistle is found on dry pasture up to 2100m altitude across the Alps, except for some central regions, and flowers July–September. The tag refers to 'white wool', describing the fluff. The massive bulbous centre is punctuated with long spines and covered with down, and the purple-red flower resembles a shaving brush. The pinnate leaves bear long spines. The main name is derived from the Greek for 'varicose', and it was used to treat varicose veins; it was also eaten, like an artichoke.

Alpine Bistort

Polygonum viviparum – Renouée vivipare –
Knöllchen-Knöterich – Poligono viviparo

A dainty inconspicuous plant
with small tufted white flowers like knots, crowded onto
a spike that is shared by tiny
brownish bulbils and slender
veined leaves. Widespread,
it flowers June–August up to
2300m altitude on grassy terrain with rocks. The tag may
derive from the plant's 'live
young' (a reference to the
bulbils); it was also reportedly
in great demand in 15th century as an antidote to snake
bites. *See also* Red: Common
Bistort.

Alpine Buttercup

Ranunculus alpestris –
Renoncule alpestre – Alpen-Hanenfuss – Ranuncolo alpestre

The five petals of this elegant pure white
buttercup are slightly notched and have
very faint veining. The glossy dark green
five-lobed leaves grow close to the
ground. Found on stony ground and in
meadows up to 3000m altitude, it flowers May–September. Similar Glacier
Crowfoot has a pink tint and is fleshier.
The genus name was probably coined
by the Roman naturalist Pliny the Elder
and comes from the Latin for 'little frog'
because many species grow in damp
places where the amphibians live.

Alpine Butterwort

Pinguicola alpina – Grassette des Alpes –
Alpen-Fettkraut – Pinguicola alpina

This insectivorous plant has wavy-edged bonnet-like white flowers with dainty yellow spots in the throat. However, the leaves, which are sticky pale green with turned-in edges, are vital insect traps. Found across the Alps in bogs and near streams up to 2600m altitude, it flowers May–August. *See also* Purple: Common Butterwort.

Alpine Mezereon, Alpine Spurge

Daphne alpina – Daphné des Alpes –
Alpen-Seidelbast – Dafne alpina

The dwarf deciduous shrub with twisted branches bears attractive sprays of four-petalled flowers that nestle amid hairy grey-green oblong leaves. The plant produces poisonous bright red berries at the end of summer. Found on limestone rock as high as 2000m in all but the north-eastern Alps, it flowers April–June. *See also* Red: Mezereon and Striped Daphne.

Alpine Moon Daisy

Leucanthemopsis alpina – Leucanthémopsis des Alpes –
Alpenmargerite – Margherita alpina

This daisy forms eye-catching splashes of white and yellow on otherwise bare terrain. Its pinnate leaves are dull green-grey and it generally hugs the ground in clumps. Found widely on short grass, moraines, scree and rocky places up to 3400m altitude, it flowers July–August. The genus name means 'white flower'.

Alpine Mouse-ear

Cerastium alpinum – Céraiste des Alpes –
Alpen-Hornkraut – Cerastio alpino

Five white notched petals with faint green veins and a green tinged centre are accompanied by small, light green-grey oval leaves. The plant tends to be ground-hugging, forming a mat. Spread across the central and eastern Alps on grassy and rock terrain up to 2850m altitude, it flowers July–August. It can be distinguished from Stitchwort which has deeper cleft petals, and Sandwort whose petals are unnotched.

Alpine Pasque Flower

Pulsatilla alpina – Pulsatille des Alpes –
Gewöhnliche Alpen-Küchenschelle – Anemone alpina

Posies of bright green fern-like leaves hold single bold white flowers with a bright yellow heart. This delicate yet mildly poisonous plant appears in springtime, often in the presence of snow – it flowers April–August. It can be found on meadows across most of the Alps up to 2700m altitude. It differs from the similar white Narcissus-flowered and Wood Anemones by its masses of very fine hairs and fern-like leaves. *See also* Yellow: Yellow Pasque Flower and Purple: Common Pasque Flower.

Asarum-leaved Bittercress

Cardamine asarifolia – Cardamine è feuilles d'asaret –
Haselwurz-Schaumkraut – Cardamine con foglie di asaro

Often found alongside mountain streams and on damp meadows, this prolific plant has large round leaves that are glossy bright green, heart shaped and slightly toothed. The small flowers are white and sport violet anthers. It flowers May–September in patches of the western and central-southern Alps up to 2000m altitude. (Asarum is a type of wild ginger with similar leaves.)

Bladder Campion

Silene vulgaris – Silène vulgaire –
Gewöhnliches Leimkraut – Silene rigonfia

This member of the Pink family has rounded white separate petals attached to swollen brown-grey veined bladders nodding on slender stems. Dubbed *schioppettino* in northern Italy from the sound it makes when popped, it is a prized springtime ingredient in risottos. It flowers June–October on rocky terrain and meadows up to 3100m altitude. *See also* Red: Moss and Rock Campion.

Burnt Orchid

Orchis ustulata – Orchis brûlé –
Brand-Knabenkraut – Orchidea bruciacchiata

A handsome orchid whose clustered flowers have a white background decorated with dark brown-purple spots and hood. The spike grows tall but the inconspicuous grass-like leaves tend to stay low. It flowers April–September on dry meadows and grassy places to 2100m altitude. *See also* Orchids: Musk and Small White; Red: Bee and Black Vanilla; Yellow: Elder-flowered and Lady's Slipper; Purple: Broad-leaved Marsh, Common Spotted and Heath Spotted.

Christmas Rose

Helleborus niger – Ellébore noir –
Gewöhnliche Christrose – Rosa di natale

Armed with a stout fleshy stem, the saucer-like flower has large white petals with yellow anthers, rather like the Alpine Pasque Flower. Found over most of the central-eastern Alps up to 1900m altitude, it flowers February–May. The 'dark' tag refers to the colour of the root tuber. Hellebore comes from 'eliminate food' as it is toxic. According to Hippocrates it was used widely in ancient Greece for treating madness and constipation. In 600BC the Athenians beseiged Kirra and poisoned the inhabitants by putting the plant into the river water. One of the earliest to burst through wintery ground, it was ostensibly the only flower a poor shepherd could find to take as homage to baby Jesus, hence its common names. *See also* Green Hellebore.

Ciliate Rock-jasmine

Androsace villosa – Androsace velue –
Zottiger Mannschild – Androsace villosa

A rare flower of great beauty that grows in the far eastern and southern Alps, this hardy cushion plant with rounded leaf rosettes has eye-catching white blooms with a red or yellow eye. It flowers June–August up to 3000m altitude, mostly on limestone rock and screes. The genus name originates from 'man' and 'shield' due to the shape of the rosettes, whereas the tag refers to the dense fine 'hairs' on the plant.

Common Cottongrass

Eriophorum angustifolium – Linaigrette à feuilles étroites –
Schmalblättiges Wollgras – Erioforo a foglie strette

While not strictly a flower, it is a common sight throughout the Alps up to 2500m altitude – tiny sails in a sea of lush green. Several dishevelled soft cotton wool heads share a stem, unlike the solitary heads of Scheuchzer's Cottongrass. A lover of watery environments such as boggy terrain, marshes and stream edges, it serves as a handy warning of wet boots for walkers! It is at its peak June–August. The genus means 'bearer of wool' and the tag 'narrow leaved'.

Common Eyebright

Euphrasia rostkoviana – Euphraise de Rostkov –
Wiesen-Augentrost – Eufrasia di Rostkov

Also called *Euphrasia officinalis*, this short, slightly hairy plant tinged with red proliferates in stony places as well as in meadows and woods July–October up to 3000m altitude. Partly parasitic, its tiny delicate white flowers with outstretched lower lobes have a hint of lilac and a yellow throat. The plant is well known for its soothing properties for eyes, as reflected in different language names. Euphrosyne was the Greek goddess of joy, while the tag honours an 18th-century Prussian naturalist.

Common Solomon's Seal

Polygonatum multiflorum – Polygonate multiflore –
Veilblütiges Salomonssiegel – Sigillo di Salomone multifloro

The attractive plant sports small clusters of drooping elongated bell-like flowers aligned down the stem opposite oval ribbed glossy green leaves. The white flowers may be either veined or tipped with green. It flowers April–June in woods up to 2200m altitude. Freckle removal, anti-inflammatory poultices and haemorrhoid treatment are but three examples of the plant's vast applications in ancient herbal medicine. However, the intriguing name refers to circular scars left on the tuber once the plant dies off, like the magic ring-cum-seal of King Solomon.

Dog's Tooth Violet

Erythronium dens-canis –
Érythrone dent de chien – Hundszahnlilie – Dente di cane

This spectacular and widespread wood dweller has white or reddish purple winged flowers that resemble helicopters. The plant, a member of the Lily family, owes its common name to the bulbs shaped like canine teeth while the genus derives from the Greek 'red' for the stem. It flowers March–May up to 2000m altitude across the southern Alps and in large pockets in the east and west.

Edelweiss

Leontopodium alpinum – Étoile des Alpes – Edelweiss – Stella alpina

Dull white felty bracts like petals surround the tufted yellow flowerheads. Stalks and elongated leaves are woody and hairy, and the plant keeps a low profile. Found across the Alps on pasture and rocky terrain up to 3500m altitude, it flowers July–September. The genus means 'lion's foot' due to the root shape. Drab appearance notwithstanding, this is the most famous alpine flower and the subject of legends (see Naming section of the Introduction). It enjoys huge popularity as a symbol for everything from beer to troops, and was immortalised in *The Sound of Music*. Once gathered by generations, it is now protected.

Glacier Crowfoot

Ranunculus glacialis – Renoncule des glaciers – Gletscher-Hahnenfuss – Ranunculo dei ghiacciai

This buttercup has short fleshy stems and rounded yellow-centred flowers that start out white and progessively assume pinkish hues, distinguishing it from the similar Alpine Buttercup. The glossy dark green leaves are three-lobed, though forked leaves grow immediately below the flowers. The plant hugs the ground amid moraines and screes, often near snow. Widespread, it holds the Alpine plant record for altitude, at 4274m on the Finsteraarhorn in the Swiss Alps, and flowers July–August.

Goatsbeard Spiraea

Aruncus dioicus – Aronce dioïque – Wald-Geissbart – Barba di capra

The common bushy plant has masses of foliage and long multi-branched stalks whose spiky ends are covered with tiny white blossoms, forming a pyramid. It loves damp shady woods, and flowers May–August up to 1700m altitude. The genus name means 'goat's beard' while the tag explains that male and female reproductive organs are borne on separate flowering spikes.

Grass of Parnassus

Parnassia palustris – Parnassia palustre – Studentenröschen – Parnassia palustre

What an inspirational name! Parnassus was the garden of the gods for the ancient Greeks, a place of great beauty. A little like a buttercup, the unpretentious solitary flowers are white with delicate light green veining while its leaves are basal and heart-shaped. It flowers June–September in marshes and damp grassy areas across the Alps as high as 2500m altitude.

Greater Stitchwort

Stellaria holostea – Stellaire holostée –
Grossblumige Sternmiere – Stellaria olostea

Easily confused with prostrate
Alpine Mouse-ear, this is a
taller plant with deeper clefts
in the five white petals as well
as pairs of long pointed leaves
that grow at right angles out
of a squarish stem. Found in
woods across the north-east
and southern Alps up to 2000m
altitude, it flowers April–June.
In combination with acorns
and wine, it is on record as an
effective cure for lumbago.

Great Masterwort, Mountain Sanicle

Astrantia major – Grande astrance –
Grosse Sterndolde – Astranzia maggiore

Perfectly symmetrical flowers that are showy
stars – hence the genus name – this tall plant
can grow up to a metre tall. The blooms are
basically white but
have green tips,
pink centres and
bushy stamens. It
is found in mead-
ows and woods
across the Alps
up to 2000m alti-
tude and flowers
June–August.

Green Hellebore

Helleborus viridus – Ellébore vert –
Grüne Nieswurz –Elleboro verde

A late winter flowerer, this unassuming but attractive plant appears in woods once the snow has melted. Its sizeable leaves resemble skinny hands, and the large open cup-shaped flowers of pale green, with evident white stamens, turn downwards when fully open. Distributed in patches across the Alps, it flowers February–April as high as 1600m altitude. *See also* Christmas Rose.

Intermediate Wintergreen

Pyrola media – Pyrole intermédiare –
Mittleres Wintergrun – Piroletta intermedia

Small drooping cup flowers of a creamy or pinkish colour hang off a light brown stalk rising from round shiny light green leaves. It flowers June–August on moors and woodlands to 2200m altitude over all but the southern Alps. The genus name derives from 'pear', most likely because of the shape of the leaves. The plant cohabits with a fungus that envelops its rhizome and in exchange supplies the plant with mineral salts and nitrogen.

Julian Poppy

Papaver julicum – Pavot d'Ernest Mayer –
Ernest Mayers Alpen-Mohn – Papavero delle Alpi Giulie

This pretty white poppy with papery petals is much less common than the better known yellow Rhaetian Poppy as it is endemic to the Julian Alps in the far south-east. Dedicated to a botanist from Ljubljana, it flowers July–August on rocky ground and screes up to 2600m altitude.

Lady's Mantle

Alchemilla vulgaris – Alchèmille commune –
Spitzlappige Frauenmantel – Alchemilla vulgaris

Small clusters of green-yellow blooms appear between outspread fan-shaped toothed leaves, often dripping with water drops expelled by the plant. This was highly prized by alchemists for transforming metals into gold, a feasible explanation of the genus name. The leaves have a multitude of applications in herbal medicine from sedative to antibacterial. Widespread, it flowers June–September in damp meadows and clearings up to 3100m altitude.

Larch Leaf Sandwort

Minuartia laricifolia – Minuartie à feuilles de mélèze –
Lärchenblättrige Miere – Minuartia con foglie di larice

Dainty white flowers of five separate petals with longish stamens and a delicate yellow centre form a cup shape. The thin stems branch towards the top to bear several blooms. It flowers July–August on rocks and screes up to 2000m altitude. The genus was dedicated to an 18th-century Spanish doctor and botanist. As the tag suggests, the leaves resemble larch needles. Its unnotched petals set it apart from the similar Alpine Mouse-ear.

Lax Potentilla

Potentilla caulescens – Potentille caulescente –
Stängel-Fingerkraut – Potentilla caulescente

Clusters of small white flowers cascade out of limestone fissures. Five petals are set around a creamy-greenish centre with light green stamens. Its faintly hairy leaves resemble the fingers of an outstretched hand. It flowers widely July–September up to 2400m altitude. *Potentilla* derives from 'resilient', and was the term chosen by Renaissance botanists to emphasise its medicinal qualities and success in colonising. *See also* Red: Pink Cinquefoil and Yellow: Golden Cinquefoil.

Lesser Butterfly Orchid

Platanthera bifolia – Platanthère à deux feuilles –
Weisse Waldhyazinthe – Platantera a fiori bianchi

This attractive white orchid with yellowy shades emanates a vanilla scent that proves irresistible to butterflies and moths whose long thin feeding apparatus gives them easy access to the plant's delicious nectar. The plant has a pair of broad basal leaves that are shiny and faintly ribbed. It grows widely across the Alps in both meadows and woods as high as 2300m altitude, and blooms May–July. It differs from the similar Greater Butterfly Orchid (not illustrated here) which has greener flowers and no scent at all.

Mossy Saxifrage

Saxifraga broides – Saxifrage faux bryum –
Moos-Steinbrech – Sassifraga brioide

Delicate creamy blooms with yellow markings grow singly on a reddish stem. A robust plant, its tiny spiky leaves form mats over rock surfaces and in crannies. Widespread across the Alps, it grows happily up to 4000m altitude but only flowers July–August. *See also* Paniculate, Starry and Thickleaved Saxifrage; Red: Two-flowered Saxifrage; Yellow: Yellow Mountain Saxifrage.

Mountain Avens

Dryas octopetala – Dryade à huit pétales –
Silberwurz – Camedrio alpino

A hardy evergreen pioneer plant that colonises moraine ridges, it forms ground-hugging carpets of oblong toothed leaves that have a silvery woolly underside. The flowers comprise a yellow centre surrounded by eight (or sometimes seven) showy white petals, as suggested by the tag. The genus derives from the Greek for 'oak' due to the shape of the leaves. It also grows in dry meadows to 2500m altitude and flowers June–August across the Alps.

Musk Milfoil

Achillea moschata – Achillée musquée –
Moschus-Scharfgarbe – Achillea moscata

Bright green feathery leaves grow down the multi-branched stalk topped with clusters of whitish-creamy petals around a very pale yellow disk. Widespread across most of the Alps, it flowers June–August on stony terrain up to 3500m altitude. The namesake for this genus, the Greek hero Achilles, was familiar with its medicinal properties and used it to treat wounded companions during the Trojan War. *See also* Silvery Milfoil.

Musk Orchid

Herminium monorchis –
Herminium à un tubercule – Einorchis – Orchidea ad un bulbo

An uncommon orchid remarkably hard to spot as it blends in with its surroundings, it has minuscule green-yellow blooms that are clustered loosely around the top of the spike. Scented honey-musk, it flowers May–August in dry meadows and at the edge of woods to 1800m altitude. *See also* Orchids: Burnt and Small White; Red: Bee and Black Vanilla; Yellow: Elder-flowered and Lady's Slipper; Purple: Broad-leaved Marsh, Common Spotted and Heath Spotted.

Nailwort

Paronychia kapela – Paronychia de la Kapela –
Kapela-Nagelkraut – Paronichia della Kapela

Curious translucent 'fingernails' distinguish this creeping plant. The actual flowers, tiny open cups, are lime green with bright yellow anthers. It flowers May–July in damp places up to 2400m altitude and is restricted to the south-western Alps and a small pocket in the south-east – thus the tag *kapela*, a mountainous area in Croatia. The genus name is derived from the Greek for 'nail-like', and it was also reputed to cure a fingernail ailment.

Narcissus-flowered Anemone

Anemone narcissifolia – Anénome à fleur de narcisse –
Narzissenblütige Anemone – Anemone con fiori di narciso

Masses of dainty white five-petalled flowers with a yellow heart sprout in bright groups from a bed of leaves. Thickets are common, giving the appearance of bushes. Its hairlessness and deeply cut palmate leaves distinguish it from similar Pasque Flowers (whose leaves are fern-like) and the flimsy Three-leaved Anemone. The name comes from the Greek 'wind' as the petals are easily blown away. Widespread, it flowers May–July in woods up to 1900m altitude.

Net-leaved Willow

Salix reticulata – Saule à réseau – Netz-Weide – Salice reticolata

This prostrate dwarf willow grips rock faces and screes and hugs the ground, forming mats. Its flattish, round leaves are grey-green and downy under-neath, while its upright catkins are modest and reddish. It flow-

ers June–August up to 2500m altitude. Found across the Alps, it grows ever so slowly, with networks of slender roots and branches that creep over rock surfaces, acting as anchors. *Salix* may derive from Celtic for 'close to water'. *See also* similar Retuse-leaved Willow, distin-guishable by its oblong leaves.

One-flowered Fleabane

Erigeron uniflorus – Vergerette à une tête –
Einköpfiges Berufkraut – Erigeron unifloro

Dubbed a 'flower with a vocation' from the medieval idea that a vocation inferred a curse, this plant was the antidote. Rather plain-looking, its dull white-pink flowers have shorn-off rays circling a bright yellow centre, and the older the plant, the darker the flowers. It lives on rocky terrain as well as in grass and flowers July–September up to 3000m altitude across the Alps, often near snow.

Paniculate Saxifrage, Livelong Saxifrage

Saxifraga paniculata – Saxifrage paniculée –
Trauben-Steinbrech – Sassifraga panicolata

Slender green-yellowish stems bear an upright panicle, a cluster of creamy-white five-petalled blooms. The oval leaves are finely toothed and arranged in showcase basal rosettes, recognisable by their lime encrustations. Widespread, it grows on rocks as high as 2700m altitude, and flowers May–August. *See also* Mossy, Starry and Thick-leaved Saxifrage; Red: Two-flowered Saxifrage; Yellow: Yellow Mountain Saxifrage; Purple: Purple Saxifrage.

Parsley Fern

Criptogramma crispa – Cryptogramma crispée –
Krauser Rollfarn – Felcetta crespa

A type of rock-brake fern, this has lacy-edged fronds like parsley and is widely distributed at well over 2000m altitude. It seeks out cool damp places to grow, usually under rocks, true to its genus name which derives from 'hidden' and 'curly'. It reaches its peak June–August.

Pheasant's-eye Narcissus, Poet's Narcissus

Narcissus poeticus – Narcisse des poètes –
Dichter-Narzisse – Narciso selvatico

Spring visitors will cherish the sight of meadows transformed into a scented white sea by zillions of these fragile flowers. Large and showy, they have six pure white petals surrounding an orange-rimmed yellow eye. They flower April–May in patches across the central and western Alps up to 2300m altitude. According to Pliny the genus name comes from the Greek for 'torpor' due to the flower's intense perfume; however, for Linnaeus it may well have been the flower that inspired the tale of Narcissus, the vain youth punished by the gods and transformed into the bloom.

Prickly Drypis

Drypis spinosa – Drypis de Jacquin –
Jacquins Kronenkraut – Dripide comune

The curious and sizeable
woody dome-shaped plant
produces sprays of star-shaped
flowers amid a sea of thorns.
A rarity, it is endemic to the
south-eastern corner of Alps
where it grows on loose scree
and slopes of broken rock up
to 2500m altitude. The flowers can be either white or
pale pink, and they appear
June–July.

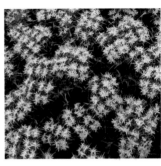

Retuse-leaved Willow, Stunted Willow

Salix retusa – Salice è feuilles émoussées –
Stumpfblättrige Weide – Salice retusa

The multi-branched and
spreading prostrate woody
plant bears light green-yel-
low-reddish catkin flowers
that are upright and straggly,
while the seeds are downy.
The shiny green oblong leaves
distinguish it from the Net-
leaved Willow, which has
round leaves. It flowers May–
September and grows widely
up to 3000m altitude.

St Bernard's Lily

Anthericum liliago – Anthéricum à fleurs de lis –
Astlose Graslilie – Lilioasfodelo maggiore

This delicate lily has six slender petals in a star formation, whereas the similar St Bruno's Lily is trumpet shaped. The tall plant has low inconspicuous leaves like grass. It flowers May–June on dry pasture and rocky terrain up to 1800m altitude in the central and west Alps. The genus name derives from the Greek for 'spike', whereas the common name honours a 12th-century French saint.

St Bruno's Lily

Paradisea liliastrum – Paradisie faux lis –
Weisse Trichterlilie – Giglio di monte

Larger and showier than St Bernard's Lily, this has six broad petals which form a trumpet. Found across the southern and north-west Alps, it flowers June–July on meadows up to 2500m altitude and may have been named in honour of the 19th-century Italian senator Paradisi. The common English name is a reference to the founder of the 11th-century monastic order of Carthusians, based in the French Alps.

Scheuchzer's Cottongrass

Eriophorum scheuchzeri – Linaigrette de Scheuchzer –
Scheuchzers Wollgras – Erioforo di Scheuchzer

A single tousled cottony head to a single stem sets this apart from the multi-branched Common Cottongrass. Forming vast green and white meadows, it blooms in marshes and along the banks of alpine lakes and streams June–August up to 2800m altitude. The genus means 'bearer of wool', describing the flowerhead, while the tag is homage to an 18th-century Swiss botanist.

Silvery Milfoil

Achillea clavennae – Achillée de Clavena –
Clavenas Schafgarbe – Achillea di Clavena

Clusters of simple white flowers, each with an off-white central disc, are clustered at the top of a multi-branched stalk. It can be distinguished from the similar Musk Milfoil by its leaves, which are silvery-bluish in colour and flattish and pinnate in shape. It flowers June–August up to 2500m altitude across the eastern-central Alps on scree and rock surfaces, often on limestone. The tag is homage to the 17th-century botanist who studied it. *See also* Musk Milfoil.

Small White Orchid

Pseudorchis albida – Pseudorchis blanchâtre –
Weisse Nacktdrüse – Orchidea candida

Minuscule greenish-white-yellow waxy bells with a wider green lip cluster around the top of a slender stem. Broad leaves grow from the base. Even when the plant reaches its peak, the short blooms look as though they are not fully open. Broadly distributed, it flowers May–September on poor grassland up to 2500m altitude. *See also* Orchids: Burnt and Musk; Red: Bee and Black Vanilla; Yellow: Elder-flowered and Lady's Slipper; Purple: Broad-leaved Marsh, Common Spotted and Heath Spotted.

Spring Pasque Flower

Pulsatilla vernalis – Pulsatille du printemps –
Frühlings-Küchenschelle – Anemone primaverile

This beautiful anemone comes bursting out of the ground even without waiting for the last patch of snow to melt away. The purple-pink hue on the outside of its white veined petals distinguishes it from another early

bloomer, the Alpine Pasque Flower. The flower is a deep cup with bright yellow prominent stamen and stigma. Fleshy pinnate leaves stay close to the ground. Fine hairs cover the plant. Found on stony terrain and meadows across the Alps up to 3600m altitude, it flowers March–July. *See also* Pasque Flowers Yellow: Yellow and Purple: Common.

Snowdrop

Galanthus nivalis – Perce-neige –
Schneeglöckchen – Bucaneve

A herald of spring, these delicate drooping bells hang from a bluish stem. Pure white outside and with the innermost petals edged with dark green, this distinguishes it from the similar Snowflake. The genus name comes from the Greek for 'milk' and 'flower', while *nivalis* refers to its appearance amid snow. According to legend an angel sent to comfort Eve in exile from the Garden of Eden created the flower from a snowflake as a symbol of hope. The plant was introduced to England from Italy during Elizabethan times. It flowers February–April in damp meadows and woods up to 1600m altitude across the Alps, except for the south-west and parts of the central and eastern regions.

Spring Snowflake

Leucojum vernum – Nivéole du printemps –
Märzglöckchen – Campanellino di primavera

Similar to the Snowdrop, this elegant solitary nodding flower has a billowing skirt and clearly visible light green-yellow spots on the tips of all the petals. Found throughout the Alps except for the far western corner, it thrives in damp woods and meadow edges up to 1600m and flowers February–April. The genus name probably comes from the Greek for 'white violet', while the tag refers to its flowering period: spring.

Starry Saxifrage

Saxifraga stellaris – Saxifrage étoilée –
Sternblütiger Steinbrech – Sassifraga stellata

Tiny five-pointed star flowers on long slender branched stems, each petal of this delightfully delicate bloom has two minuscule yellow spots. Found on damp terrain or alongside streams, it flowers May–August up to 2600m altitude. *See also* Mossy, Paniculate and Thick-leaved Saxifrage; Red: Two-flowered Saxifrage; Yellow: Yellow Mountain Saxifrage; Purple: Purple Saxifrage.

Stemless Carline Thistle

Carlina acaulis – Carline sans tige –
Gewöhnliche Silberdistel – Carlina acaule

With spiky triffid-like leaves radiating out from a central dome, this photogenic thistle has large creamy flowers that shut up like clams in the damp. According to mountain lore, when it is closed bad weather can be expected and when the flower opens up flat to the ground, the sun will shine. The plant's namesake was the 8th-century Holy Roman Emperor Charlemagne, who fed the roots to his troops as a cure for the plague. The plant has recognised medicinal uses ranging from disinfectant to laxative, and can be eaten like an artichoke. It flowers June–September on dry meadows and rocky terrain up to 2000m altitude across the Alps except for patches in the north.

Swallow-wort

Vincetoxicum hirundinaria – Dompte-venin officinal –
Schwalbenwurz – Vincetossico comune

The tall elegant plant bears pairs of pointed lance-shaped leaves whose upper surface is glossy dark green and duller beneath. These are interspersed with with groups of five-petalled star-shaped flowers that are creamy white with a shade of green. It flowers May–August in woods and stony places up to 1800m altitude. Highly poisonous, it was formerly renowned as an antidote to snake bites, which explains the genus name 'disintoxicating'. The tag 'swallow-like' refers to the shape of the root.

Thick-leaved Saxifrage

Saxifraga callosa – Saxifrage calleuse –
Dickblättriger Steinbrech – Sassifraga meridionale

Found on limestone cliffs and sheltered rocks in the Maritime Alps, this straggly drooping plant has long stems supporting dense clusters of five-petalled white flowers. The leaves are elongated grey-green spears that grow out of the basal rosette. It flowers May–July up to 2500m altitude. *See also* Mossy, Paniculate and Starry Saxifrage; Red: Two-flowered Saxifrage; Yellow: Yellow Mountain Saxifrage; Purple: Purple Saxifrage.

Thick-leaved Stonecrop

Sedum dasyphyllum – Orpin à feuilles épaisses –
Dickblatt-Mauerpfeffer – Sedo a foglie spesse

The tiny white star flowers have occasional pink dots and a yellow centre. The curious leaves are round, fleshy, sticky and even downy. Commonly found in rock crannies on dry sunny stony terrain to 2500m altitude, it flowers June–August. The tag means 'hairy leaved'. *See also* Red: Caucasian Stonecrop and Yellow: Biting and Creamish Stonecrop.

Three-leaved Anemone

Anemone trifolia – Anémone trifoliée –
Dreiblatt-Anemone – Anemone trifogliata

Forming vast carpets in the woods, these flimsy flowers stand solitary on spindly stems. They have a much paler yellow centre than the Narcissus-flowered Anemone and are hairless, unlike the Alpine Pasque Flower. The large leaves are three-lobed and slightly toothed. It flowers May–June up to 1900m, across the central-east Alps.

Twinflower

Linnaea borealis – Linnée boréale –
Mossglöckchen – Linnea

Two small, delicate droop-ing pale pink-white bell-like blooms hang off a long forked stalk. Hailing originally from the sub-Artic regions, the plant spread south with the Ice Ages and is now found in conifer woods and marshy terrain over much of the Alps up to 2200m altitude. It flow-ers June–August and was a favourite of the great natural-ist Linnaeus.

White Butterbur

Petasites albus – Pétasite blanc – Weisse Pestwurz – Farfaraccio bianco

A prehistoric-looking plant that resembles a toilet brush, this is commonly seen in the undergrowth and on the banks of streams in springtime. The genus means 'parasol' due to its large, shading leaves, and the tag 'white'. It flow-ers March–May up to 2200m altitude across the Alps. In olden times butter would be wrapped up in its large rounded leaves, and it was also well known in herbal medicine.

White Crocus

Crocus albiflorus – Crocus à fleurs blancs –
Alpen-Frühlings-Safran – Croco bianco

These short-stalked flowers are generally pure white but may be veined and feathered with purple, while the spiky leaves have a white groove down the middle. One of the first to burst through compressed leaf litter and old grass, even in the vicinity of snow patches, they appear in spring and flower March–June. They form attractive carpets up to 2700m altitude. *See also* Purple: Meadow Saffron.

White False Helleborine

Veratrum album – Vératre blanc – Grünlicher Germer – Veratro bianco

Of striking beauty and emanating a delicate perfume, stars of six lime-green or yellow-white petals surround a light green centre. The long woody stems have elongated ribbed leaves, and prior to flowering the plant is eas-

ily confused with the Great Yellow Gentian. Given a wide berth by grazing livestock, it contains a deadly toxin that was handy in the preparation of poison-tipped spears for ancient battles. It flowers June–August in damp clearings and meadows up to 2700m altitude in the central and southern Alps.

White Rockrose

Helianthemum apenninum – Hélianthème des Apennins –
Apenninen-Sonnenröschen – Eliantemo degli Appennini

Despite the tag, this Rockrose is found across the south-western and south-central Alps. A low-growing shrub, it sports frail white paper-like flowers on narrow stems. The narrow leaves are dull bluish-grey, a bit like Rosemary in shape. It grows on grassy and stony terrain up to 1800m and flowers April–June. The genus derives from the Greek for 'sun' and 'flower', due either to the colour of the flower or the widespread belief that it lasts but a single day or opens up with the sunshine.

Wild Strawberry

Fragaria vesca – Fraisier des bois – Wald-Erdbeere –
Fragolina di bosco

Large three-lobed leaves accompany the dainty white flowers. Found commonly on grassy terrain and woods up to 2400m altitude, it flowers April–July after which the sweet fruit appears. The genus name was in use in Roman times but it can be traced back to a Sanskrit term for the fragrance of the fruit. The tag means 'soft'. Rich in vitamins, minerals and sugars, it provided many a feast for prehistoric man.

BOTANICAL GARDENS ACROSS THE ALPS

A selection of Alpine Botanical Gardens is listed here with their location and contact details. Note: they are only open during the summer months.

Austria

Innsbruck: Alpen Garten Patscherkofel
www.uibk.ac.at/bot-garden

Montafon: Alpen-Steingarten bei der Lindauer Hütte
www.alpenverein-lindau.de.
Click on 'Lindauer Hütte'

Rax Alpe: Alpengarten Rax www.raxalpe.com.
Click on 'Schutzhütte Ottohaus'

Reutte in Tirol: Alpenblumengarten an Hahnenkamm
www.alpenblumengarten.com/home.html

Villacher Alpe: Alpengarten Villacher Alpe
www.alpengarten-villach.at

France

Colle Piccolo San Bernardo: Giardino Botanico Alpino Chanousia
www.chanousia.org

Grenoble: Station Alpine Joseph Fourier http://sajf.ujf-grenoble.fr

Samoëns: Jardin La Jaysinia
http://haute-savoie.ialpes.com/jardins/la-jaysinia.html

Italy

Agordo: Giardino Botanico Alpino A. Segni del Rifugio Vazzoler
http://giardinibotanici.venetoagricoltura.org.
Click on 'Monte Civetta'

Bobbio Pellice: Giardino Botanico Alpino B Peyronel
www.tpellice.it/vpellice/tur/per/giar/intro.htm

Bormio: Giardino Botanico Rezia
http://reteortibotanicilombardia.it.
Click on 'Gli Orti della Rete'

Courmayeur: Giardino Botanico Alpino Saussurea
www.saussurea.net

Monte Baldo: Orto Botanico Novezzina
www.ortobotanicomontebaldo.org

Nevegal: Giardino botanico alpino del Monte Faverghera
http://giardinibotanici.venetoagricoltura.org.
Click on 'Monte Faverghera'

Terme di Valdieri: Giardino Botanico Valderia
www.parcoalpimarittime.it.
Click on 'Points of Interest'

Valnontey: Giardino Alpino Paradisia www.pngp.it.
Click on 'Visit the Park'

Slovenia

Val Trenta: Juliana Alpine Botanical Garden
www2.pms-lj.si/info/juliana_en.pdf

Switzerland

Adelboden: Alpengarten Höreli www.adelboden.ch.
Click on 'Attractions'

Aletsch: Alpengarten Aletsch www.pronatura-aletsch.ch

Brülisau: Alpengarten Hoher Kasten
www.hoherkasten.ch/gipfelerlebnisse/alpengarten.html

Champex: Jardin Botanique Alpin Flore-Alpe www.flore-alpe.ch

Col du Grand-Saint-Bernard:
www.unige.ch/sciences/biologie/plantsciences/linnaea

Davos: Alpinum Schatzalp www.alpinum.ch

Interlaken: Botanischer Alpengarten Schynige Platte
www.alpengarten.ch

Lausanne: Jardin Alpin La Thomasia www.botanique.vd.ch

Montreux: Jardin Alpin La Rambertia
www.bgci.org/garden.php?id=600

Oberdorf: Juragarten Weissenstein www.sac-weissenstein.ch.
Click on 'Diverses'

FLOWER INDEX

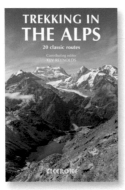
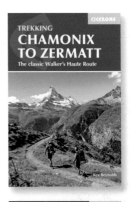
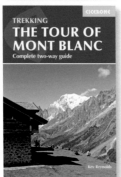
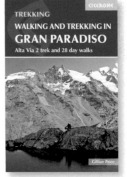

Explore the world with Cicerone

walking • trekking • mountaineering • climbing • mountain biking • cycling • via ferratas • scrambling • trail running • skills and techniques

For over 50 years, Cicerone have built up an outstanding collection of nearly 400 guides, inspiring all sorts of amazing experiences.

www.cicerone.co.uk – where adventures begin

- Our **website** is a treasure-trove for every outdoor adventurer. You can buy books or read inspiring articles and trip reports, get technical advice, check for updates, and view videos, photographs and mapping for routes and treks.

- **Register this book** or any other Cicerone guide in your member's library on our website and you can choose to automatically access updates and GPX files for your books, if available.

- Our **fortnightly newsletters** will update you on new publications and articles and keep you informed of other news and events. You can also follow us on Facebook, Twitter and Instagram.

We hope you have enjoyed using this guidebook. If you have any comments you would like to share, please contact us using the form on our website or via email, so that we can provide the best experience for future customers.

CICERONE

Juniper House, Murley Moss Business Village, Oxenholme Road, Kendal LA9 7RL

✉ info@cicerone.co.uk   cicerone.co.uk 🇫🇧🐦📷